Peer Support Works

A step by step guide to long term success

Netta Cartwright

network
continuum

Published by Network Continuum Education
The Tower Building
11 York Road
London
SE1 7NX

www.networkcontinuum.co.uk
www.continuumbooks.com

An imprint of The Continuum International Publishing Group Ltd

First published 2007
© Netta Cartwright 2007

ISBN-13:   978 1 85539 166 6
ISBN-10:   1 85539 166 X

For Kate and Tom

Layout by: Neil Hawkins, ndesignuk.co.uk

Printed in Great Britain by MPG Books Ltd, Bodmin, Cornwall

Contents

Introduction

Never doubt that a small group of committed citizens can change the world; indeed it's the only thing that ever has.

(Margaret Mead)

This book provides a user-friendly manual to establish and sustain peer support programmes in the learning environment. It has been written specifically with practitioners in mind, offering down to earth advice based on many years of first-hand experience. Over recent years teachers have become increasingly interested in the idea of peer support for their students. They see it as a means of proactively preventing and tackling problems in their schools. Peer support has been set up in many schools across the United Kingdom and is becoming commonplace. It has established itself with a successful track record.

Accompanying this growth have been many reports outlining successful practice and manuals with guidelines on how to set it up. Until now the emphasis has by necessity been on how to initiate peer support schemes. There has been less information on how they can be sustained over the longer term. Now that many schools have kept up the momentum of their schemes for many years, we can learn from their experience.

This manual focuses on the sustainability of peer support programmes. It provides information for busy practitioners and policy makers on how to initiate and continue the process. It is not dictating specific policies and practices in a formula to fit all circumstances. Instead it presents ideal conditions for peer support while recognizing that these can never be fully achieved. Each school has its own unique starting point and set of needs.

The book reflects the beauty of peer support as a process based on young people's natural wish to help each other. Even in the most difficult circumstances where very few of the ideal conditions are present, peer support can work wonders in a school because of the commitment of young people involved and their adult allies.

In a format that can be browsed and dipped into, this book covers three main stages to successful programmes:

- understanding peer support
- training courses
- making the programmes work in the long term.

The first section provides an overview of the history, background, theory, process, range and long term benefits of peer support. The second section provides practical advice, ideas and course plans on how to set up a variety of programmes. The third section covers sustainability, assessment, evaluation, monitoring, child protection, supervision and accreditation with examples of good practice. There are also appendices with lists of further reading, government initiatives, resources, and organizations in the field.

Peer support can make a significant difference in schools. Readers using the framework in this manual can be part of this important movement for education improvement. By setting up and sustaining peer support they can contribute to the quality of experience in schools for all young people.

Stage 1
Understanding peer support

Definition, history and background of peer support

The range of peer support models, their present scope and future potential

Theories and research evidence on peer support projects in schools

Chapter 1

Definition, history and background of peer support

> Peer support begins with the natural willingness of most young people to act in a co-operative, friendly way towards one another. Peer support systems build on this intrinsic quality and create structures which facilitate the young person's potential for responsibility, sensitivity and empathic caring.
>
> (Cowie and Sharp 1996)

What is peer support ?

The *Oxford English Dictionary* defines a peer as 'an equal in ability, standing, age etc'. People have various components to their identities such as age, gender, ethnicity, social class, sexual orientation; family role; occupation; or certain experiences such as drug taking, bereavement and separated parents. Peer support can take place between people where there is a sense of being peers in any of these ways, and as circumstances change this relationship can change over time.

A good working definition of peer support in schools is:

> .... using the knowledge, skills and experience of children and young people in a planned and structured way to understand, support, inform and help develop the skills, understanding, confidence and self-awareness of other children and young people with whom they have something in common.
>
> (Hartley-Brewer 2002)

Peer support is a generic term that includes a range of approaches and different types of projects in a variety of settings. In schools they all involve children and young people working with others to help them learn and develop emotionally, socially or academically so they can reach their full potential. These approaches focus on practices where students are trained in various skills in order to enhance pastoral care by assisting other students and knowing when to refer to professionals. However, a main benefit of peer supporters is their ability to provide the empathy, understanding and practical support needed to resolve a wide range of problems without being referred to teachers or other professionals. The advantages are manifold: students are helped with problems they would not normally refer to adults; peers can offer help that is often more appropriate and effective than adults; these problems are dealt with before crisis point; peer supporters can act as a bridge towards adult help; and teachers' time is saved so they can deal with the most serious problems.

Why do schools need peer support?

Peer support provides a mechanism for students to help each other in the school context. At its heart is the co-operation and friendliness natural to human beings. The belief that young people are intrinsically well disposed towards each other is the driving force behind the increasingly popular practice to train school students to support their peers. By training them in listening, mentoring and teaching skills, schools seek to strengthen pastoral care so that levels of security and well-being for students are improved.

Different schools have different reasons for adopting peer support. As well as providing support for students, some schools set up peer support to present information in new ways to improve young people's ability to listen and learn. Others aim to promote personal social skills and knowledge for both the givers and users of peer support. Another reason is to provide a transition point between students with problems and professional help and some schools see peer support as influencing a positive emotional ethos.

Some students may not ask adults for help because age and status gaps can act as barriers to communication. Le Surf and Lynch's (1999) consultations with young people found that in relationships with adults they believed they were 'ignored, patronized, misunderstood, disbelieved, dismissed, directed or punished'. For some young people this negative view may extend to counsellors, whose professional role may be perceived as impersonal help, or even as another authority figure telling them what to do. Peers can offer something distinctive to each other. They have experiences in common and can empathize with others in distress and research has shown that peer-led interventions are better able to engage young people than adult support. Peers demonstrate closer understanding of the particular concerns they face, can have greater credibility and approachability, and may be more readily and regularly available, with the potential to offer support outside of formal situations.

Pupils like having a peer support service as it makes them feel safe and supported. This is a common response from Year 7 students in projects in Stafford, Tamworth and Stoke-on-Trent schools led by Netta Cartwright. Even if they never use it for problem solving they like to know it is there and they enjoy contact with the peer mentors anyway. One boy from Wolstanton High School (see Chapter 2, Case Study 7 and Chapter 10, Case Study 7) wrote, ' I like the members of the BULLYinc team because most of them I made very close friends'.

Pupils primarily like being peer supporters because they enjoy helping others and taking a responsible role in school. In a Childline project a peer mentor reflecting on her experience said, 'My greatest reward as a mentor has been putting smiles back on sad faces – and becoming a "big sister" to so many younger children. It is a wonderful thing to be trusted' (Moldrich and Carpentieri 2005). Peers supporting each other is not entirely motivated by altruism, however. Research has shown that peer supporters stand to gain long-term social benefits such as an enhanced reputation, increased self-esteem and the development of transferable interpersonal skills. Schools and the individuals within them also benefit from reductions in bullying and a school culture promoting greater emotional well-being (Glover and Cartwright 1998).

Problems are an inevitable part of school life. As a deputy head told Childline, 'any school that says it doesn't have bullying, or doesn't have discipline issues, or (at the secondary level) doesn't have kids taking drugs – well they want their heads looking at' (Moldrich and Carpentieri 2005). Peer support does not eradicate these problems but it does enable students to seek help with problems in their early stages, and before they develop into a crisis, or long term problems such as self-harm, school refusing or mental health illness as adults.

The division of labour with a shift towards student responsibility and decision making can enhance student–teacher relationships and spread the burden of dealing with minor problems and disputes. Busy teachers spend a great deal of time resolving minor conflicts among students, which takes time away from their regular teaching. With schools promoting their anti-bullying policies children are more ready to report minor incidents which all have to be dealt with. It does help if peer supporters can deal with some of these problems, and in many instances they are better suited for the work. However, just as teachers and teaching assistants need support and supervision in pastoral work so do the peer supporters – and the service will flounder without it.

Background and history

Peer support as simply people helping other people has been around since the beginning of human life, and real and fictional examples can be found in centuries of worldwide history, mythology and literature.

In the United Kingdom an early type of formal peer support was evident in the Monitorial System of Bell and Lancaster, the nineteenth-century philanthropists. They used older students to instruct younger ones as part of their project to bring education at a low cost to the masses (McGowan 2002). Monitors were seen as better able to relate to their peers than teachers because of their age. They themselves benefited, their students' behaviour improved and crime was reduced. Bell claimed that this monitorial system cultivated children's best dispositions by teaching them to take an interest in the welfare of others. The British school system kept this tradition alive with the prefect system but the practice varied in focus and tended more towards a type of policing rather than a support of younger students.

Since the 1960s peer support as it is now known developed as a movement, beginning in North America and spreading across the world. It origins were in humanistic psychology developed in the 1940s and 1950s as a 'third force' distinct from psychoanalysis and behaviourism, and evolving from the group dynamics and existentialism of the West and secular humanism of the East (Rowan 1976). (See Chapter 3 for a more detailed account of these theories and approaches.)

Applications of this psychology were Carl Rogers' person-centred counselling (Rogers 1957) and Harvey Jackins' co-counselling movement (Jackins 1965). Their belief in the inherent goodness of human beings and their capacity to self-heal were in contrast to more traditional approaches. For example, psychoanalysis assumes that human antisocial behaviour is intrinsic, inevitable and open only to partial alleviation. Jackins' Re-evaluation Counselling (RC) movement and its offshoot, Co-Counselling International, developed worldwide peer counselling networks beyond the sphere of professional counselling. In the 1950s Jackins and his associates experimented with taking turns as counsellor and client. They discovered that ordinary people exchanging attention in this way could help each other recover from hurtful experiences in life, even the most severe and prolonged (Kauffman and New 2004). By practising co-counselling people 'learn how to re-discover their natural ability to give and get good attention from one another through basic listening skills. These skills are then used on a structured basis whereby, through mutual consent, people of all ages and backgrounds assist one another in co-counselling sessions to "discharge" [emotions] confidentially and free themselves from the damaging effects of old hurts' (Cartwright 1996).

Other peer support practices and networks have either followed or simultaneously developed to become a movement offering a variety of structured models to strengthen what friends have to offer, thereby increasing a person's ability to find safe and satisfying solutions to problems. In Canada and the USA the peer mentoring movement has grown since the 1970s and in Europe peer counselling and mediation were beginning to be introduced in the mid 1980s, mostly in educational settings. Similar practices were growing elsewhere, such as Australia, and are now established across the world in schools, universities, colleges, hospitals, clinics, community and recreation centres, senior citizen agencies, telephone hotlines, unions, businesses and corporations.

With the rapid expansion of peer programmes across North America, Europe and Australia a wide variety of roles developed for peers in helping each other. Programmes were developed for different ethnic and cultural groups, physical and mental health promotion, and many other special needs populations. Similar to other innovations in the helping field, the peer movement has mushroomed into many diverse practices and approaches. Reports, reviews, research and resources documenting this growth have been published in a variety of places, and this is reflected in Appendices 1, 2 and 3.

In 1985 Netta Cartwright pioneered peer support in the UK at Walton High School in Stafford when Year 11 and 12 students were taught how to co-counsel so they could support each other and younger students (Cartwright 2005). This was developed further in 1990 to be a crucial part of the school's anti-bullying policy. The Elton Report (Elton 1989) on discipline in schools endorsed this approach within the context of the UK ratification of the United Nations Convention on the Rights of Children (UNCRC). The report advocated the promotion of school environments that valued relationships and responsibility to others. Pupils were to be listened to and negotiated with about their rights and responsibilities.

Since then a small number of practitioners have set up interventions with peers helping each other. Athy Demetriades, a teacher at a London secondary school, founded Children of the Storm, a charity designed to help young refugees which included a peer partnership intervention (Demetriades 1996). The 1990s saw the growth of peer support in secondary schools primarily as anti-bullying strategies. Walton High School's programme was used as a model for peer support from 1991 to 1992 in The Sheffield Project (Sharp et al. 1994) the first and most substantive monitored intervention project in the UK. The Department of Education and Employment, in its first edition of the anti-bullying pack *Don't Suffer in Silence*, recommended peer support in schools. The current UK government is promoting peer support within the DfES citizenship and social inclusion policies. In 1995 it agreed to work within the UNCRC, which gave young people the right to participate in decisions that affect them and its continuing support is evident in the publication of *Learning to Listen: Core principles for the Involvement of children and young people* (CYPU 2002) (see Appendix 2).

In the 1990s Professor Helen Cowie at the University of Surrey convened conferences for practitioners and in 1996 started publishing the *Peer Support Networker*. In 1998 Childline launched its Childline in Partnership with Schools (CHIPS) programme, which helped schools set up peer support. In the same year a few practitioners and agencies providing peer support joined forces with Childline and the Mental Health Foundation to form the Peer Support Forum, a national body co-ordinating and promoting peer support. It became the Peer Support Network and part of the National Children's Bureau. The *Every Child Matters* (DfES 2003) policy agenda began with a Green Paper showing the government's commitment to involving young people in decisions which affect their lives, a concept at the heart of peer support. A number of organizations and training agencies across the UK now offer a variety of training courses enabling teachers and other educational workers to set up and sustain peer support in schools and other educational institutions (see Appendix 3 for websites).

Chapter 2

The range of peer support models, their present scope and future potential

 The greatest good you can do for others is not just to show your riches, but to reveal to them their own.

(Benjamin Disraeli)

The range of peer support in schools

While the peers who provide these services are united under the common theme of peers helping peers they often do so under different labels such as peer counsellors, peer listeners, peer educators, peer tutors, peer facilitators, peer mediators, peer support workers, peer helpers or peer learning assistants. This variety of applications is one of the strengths of peer support and shows how important it is to be adapted for local contexts. The principles of good practice identified by the Peer Support Forum are in the box below. They do not all need to be present for a project to be peer support but represent a standard to aim towards.

Principles of peer support (source: Peer Support Forum)

Children and young people are central to the project:
- Children and young people are provided with the skills to support each other more effectively.
- Clear objectives, boundaries and ground rules are established for all aspects of the project, after discussion and agreement with the children and young people involved.

- The self-esteem of children and young people is promoted.
- A clear, known policy and criteria are established for selecting young people who are to be peer supporters.
- There is equal access and opportunities for all children and young people to be involved in projects and/or training.

The whole community is involved:
- Projects are part of a whole-school approach which promotes a positive and supportive ethos.
- Projects involve the active commitment of more than one member of staff.
- All parents/carers are kept informed about the project and their children's participation in it.
- There is liaison with local and national agencies to support projects.

Young people receive appropriate ongoing training:
- Confidentiality (including child protection issues) as set out in the Children Act 1989 is adhered to by all involved, and covered in training and supervision.
- Projects should be regularly monitored and evaluated to ensure that objectives are being met and principles adhered to.
- Those involved in training young people must receive appropriate training and support.
- Peer supporters receive appropriate and regular supervision by trained adults.

The next section briefly outlines the range of activities and approaches across the UK, with examples of good practice according to these principles.

Befriending

Young people offer support and friendship to other young people of a similar age in everyday interactions such as helping new students or those who are lonely and helping in after-school clubs. There may be a specific focus such as bullying or the welcoming of asylum seekers. Sometimes students who have experienced similar difficulties are given the opportunity to share their experiences and feelings. Befrienders learn to understand and respect diversity as those they are befriending can often be different in some way, which may be the reason they are bullied.

Case Study 1

Kingsbury High School: a playground peer support service (Scherer-Thompson 2002)

After a year of a formal peer listening drop-in at this school, it was found that the numbers using it were low. The peer supporters replaced it with a more informal 'playground service' where any student could get regular help and support. Peer supporters using a rota system are on duty at lunchtime in the playground. They become generally known through building up relationships and actively seek out students who seem alone. They intervene in aggressive situations using their mediation skills to calm students, encourage them to listen to each other and reach agreed solutions. They keep confidential notes on events in a diary and have access to a trained staff member to discuss concerns confidentially. Two case examples were cited by Scherer-Thompson who changed the names of students to retain anonymity.

'[We] found two Year 8 pupils arguing over a broken shoe buckle. David was angry because Liam had stepped on his shoe and the buckle had broken. A crowd had started to gather... The peer supporters spoke to each in turn, calmed them, and got each one to explain what had happened while the other listened. Neither boy agreed about what the other said but they did agree to stay away from each other.'

'[We] spoke to a boy who was looking lonely. We found out that his friends were in the canteen. We talked to him and introduced ourselves and sat with him until his friends came.'

Buddy schemes

These are proactive befriending programmes designed to prevent problems occurring or escalating. They are especially suitable for primary schools where volunteer peer supporters are trained in basic listening and mediation skills so they can become buddies available to support the other children. They work mostly during break and dinner times to increase a sense of belonging and to reduce loneliness. Some schools have found that friendship benches work well, but others are concerned they may put too much attention on lonely children and prefer playground pals who encourage children to play together at breaks.

Circle of Friends

Circle of Friends (see Chapter 7) is a specific form of befriending which is practical and requiring minimal resources. It originated in North America as a means to include disabled children and adults into mainstream education and communities (Perske 1988). It is especially suitable for primary schools and has also been used with Key Stage 3 students in secondary schools. Peers volunteer to be part of a Circle of Friends for a young person who is having some kind of difficulty in her/his life. It could be the student is lonely, has behaviour problems, is bereaved or is disabled. They support and encourage the student while being supervised by an adult worker, preferably a counsellor or educational psychologist. The adult facilitator must understand the process thoroughly in order to set up the circle, and support and monitor it on a day-to-day basis. The value of this approach is its inclusive nature and how it provides the chance for a child with relationship difficulties to be seen and helped from a wide range of perspectives.

Case Study 2

Daniel – A Circle of Friends for a boy with behavioural problems (Taylor 1996)

Daniel was a Year 6 pupil in an inner city primary school. He had been excluded from his previous school and was in danger of being excluded from this one. The school's educational psychologist set up a Circle of Friends. At the initial meeting of the class without Daniel's presence, the children with the facilitator's help talked about what was good and difficult about Daniel. Also she encouraged their empathy by asking how they would feel and behave if they had no friends. This generated ideas on how they could help him and they all volunteered to be in his Circle of Friends. Six were chosen at random and met him immediately afterwards. They all agreed on various helpful approaches on the understanding that he was not their responsibility but the responsibility of the adults. Weekly follow-up meetings ensued with a structure to review what went well with these approaches, what was difficult and ideas for moving forward. After seven weeks Daniel's behaviour had improved enough for the circle to close. All the children had benefited, especially Daniel who thanked the group.

Peer advocacy

Young people identify and represent views or interests on behalf of others. This can involve speaking on behalf of others or standing by them as they represent themselves. This approach is especially useful for advocating the needs, entitlements and rights of marginalized and vulnerable young people such as those with learning disabilities (Harnett 2003).

Case Study 3

Walton High School, Staffordshire: using peer advocates in a mediation process

The school counsellor used peer advocates in a mediation process to reduce racist behaviour in a predominantly white middle class school. The conflict was between an Asian young man and two white young men. Since Year 7 the Asian boy was a victim of racist bullying from several male students in his year group. It had got worse the more he showed he was upset and retaliated by name-calling back. The head of year had tried many tactics, which had not worked. The counsellor gave separate sessions to the victim and each of the two ringleaders to enable them to think more clearly what they wanted to say in the mediation process. Each boy had a peer advocate after an initial meeting with all six to set it up. The counsellor's role was neutral facilitator and the role of each peer advocate was to support one of the boys and present his interests to the others. The Asian boy had an Asian male peer advocate and the other two each had a peer advocate who shared something in common with them. During the mediation session each boy had a turn to say what he disliked about the other two boys' behaviours and a chance to say how he felt after hearing the list of negative behaviours cited about himself. The peer advocates sat next to each of their clients to give moral support, help with their communication and speak for them if necessary. The same process was repeated with each boy saying what he had liked about the other two boys' past behaviours and how he felt about the good comments about him. Finally each boy said what behaviour he wanted from the other two and agreements were made with the help of the peer advocates. The agreements were written down and copied for each boy and the peer advocates. Weekly group sessions were arranged with the peer advocates to monitor progress. The role of the peer advocates was to check out their own clients regularly and go with them to the joint meeting. There were two or three follow-up sessions with the peer advocates and as a result the three boys got on better together for several months. It flared up again later and the disputants came as a group asking if I could set up the group meetings again. After a few more flare ups and meetings with peer advocates they settled down with no more reports of racism from the Asian boy.

Peer assessment

Assessment is an integral part of the learning processes involved in peer support. It provides the chance to identify specific learning needs as well as future needs for individuals and programmes. Peer assessment is where students assess each other's work in school. It includes peer supporters assessing each other's work in their peer support training and projects as well as students assessing each other's academic work. It is a valuable means of producing evidence of learning and can include activities such as observations of role play, checklists, interviewing each other, video or audio tapes and marking each other's work according to set criteria.

Peer counselling

This is formalized support extending the listening and mentoring approaches. It is based on a one-to-one counselling relationship. Peer supporters are trained in a wider set of counselling tools that include: active listening, reflection, empathy, verbal and non-verbal communication, confidentiality, problem solving, and self-esteem games and activities (see Chapter 5). Trained and supervised by adult counsellors and using a referral system they provide formal or informal ongoing support. This is provided on a regular basis over a period of time, in a specified room at certain times. They are not advice givers but by active listening they help to resolve bullying problems and assist individual students to find their own solutions. They may co-counsel with each other as a means of self-support and set up co-counselling clubs or support groups (Cartwright 1996). The peer counsellors can train on an accredited course from the Open College Network to levels NVQ 1 and 2, or with other accrediting bodies or agencies with their own criteria such as Childline or Re-evaluation Counselling (RC) (see Chapter 9 and Appendix 3).

Case Study 4

Rising Brook High School, Stafford: an informal drop-in and one-to-one counselling

This is a small comprehensive 11–18 school with 550 students in a working class area of a county town. In 2001 and 2002 two cohorts of Year 9 peer supporters and two staff to supervise them were trained by Netta Cartwright of Peer Support Works using the RC co-counselling model. The service they set up included a number of strategies such as a drop-in service in a specified classroom that operates every day on a rota system. Students of all ages visited the drop-in almost every day to talk to peer supporters, and it was especially useful after two tragic events took place in the school in 2003. Peer counsellors were trained and supervised by trained staff and counsellors to be part of the bereavement counselling team for students in a whole-year group.

Peer education

Peer education is the teaching of skills, attitudes and behaviours, and the imparting of information by people who are not professional trained educators.

In schools peer education means young people teaching other young people. Young people deliver presentations and teach courses to their peers on issues such as drug awareness, sexual health, bullying, conflict resolution and safe sex. It can also be formal collaborative group-work where peer supporters lead small support groups on various issues such as assertiveness, bullying or racism. Peer education extends beyond one-to-one tuition with the tutor as an expert imparting knowledge to a novice. In fact there are advantages in tutors not being expert as they understand the difficulties of learning which can be reassuring, helpful and unthreatening to the tutee. The peer educator may learn and develop as much as the tutee, both cognitively and in social abilities (Cowie and Wallace 2000).

Peer education is also based on the idea expressed by Added Power and Understanding in Sex Education (APAUSE) on their website www.ex.ac.uk/sshs/apause/peerspages.htm. 'Older teenagers are more effective than teachers and health professionals at influencing the beliefs and behaviours of younger people. They understand teenage culture and views and are best placed to appreciate the current pressures put on them by others and by society as well as their goals and aspirations. Young teenagers feel more comfortable discussing sensitive issues with someone of a similar age than with a "parental" figure. For this reason we train young people as "peer educators", enabling them to go into classrooms and deliver information on sexual health and relationships in a way that teenagers will relate to' (for more examples of peer education see Chapter 10).

Case Study 5

APAUSE in Schools - Peer led sessions on sex education (Morgan 2004)

APAUSE is a programme where students aged 16–17 are recruited from local colleges of further education and school sixth forms. They receive approximately 20 hours intensive training and further rehearsal time for each session. Each session is led by a team of three or four (where possible) mixed sex peers, involving small group-work, discussion, role play and OHP presentations. Although it is essential for a teacher to be present they do not take an active part in the delivery unless asked to do so by the peer educators. Peer educators are not expected to be able to deliver knowledge and skills on their own. They work with other peers and concentrate on helping younger teenagers understand and manage their relationships by:

- running class discussions;
- helping with small group-work;
- demonstrating and assisting with role plays;
- helping them to set up and run short scenes (See Chapter 10 for more details on APAUSE).

Peer listening

Young people learn active listening skills to provide a range of services where children have the safety to talk about minor worries to deeper concerns such as bereavement or bullying. The 'clients' have their worries taken seriously and are encouraged to find their own solutions and decide what to do. Sometimes the peer listeners work alongside younger students in extra-curricular clubs, paired reading and prefect duties. Lunchtime drop-ins are very common, often with games and activities to provide a relaxed atmosphere in addition to a quiet room for students to discuss problems one-to-one.

Peer mediation

Young people and adults are trained in mediation skills to provide a neutral conflict resolution service for others. They encourage problem solving between disputing students often around bullying issues and being part of a 'no blame' approach (see Chapter 6). Schools have found that these programmes reduce disputes, day to day quarrels, exclusions and violence. In the mediation process young people learn that they cannot coerce to get their own way. They learn to recognize the effect of conflicts on others and how they can be resolved.

Peer mentoring

Older students provide positive role models to younger students in schools. This is provided in two possible ways that often overlap. The most common is another kind of 'buddy' system where trained students are attached to a new intake group or class to befriend and guide new students into the school environment. This usually begins on the induction day for children about to start their new secondary school and continues in the first year. Another type of peer mentoring is where a peer supporter acts as mentor to one or two mentees over a limited period of time offering a supportive one-to-one friendship,

Two mediators and two disputants face each other

listening and mediation. This kind of support may be offered during a difficult time for a student. For example, a mentor may help a student returning after a long illness or bereavement. They can also offer support during transition periods or before exams.

Case Study 6

Saltley Peer Mentoring Project, Birmingham (Lepper, *Children Now* 19 April 2005)

This peer mentoring scheme, funded by the Department for Education and Skills and run by the British Red Cross and Birmingham's Saltley Secondary School, trained at-risk older children as mentors to help younger students with problems ranging from homework to bullying. Since the British Red Cross chose the school in 2003 for one of its formal mentoring schemes, six local businesses were brought in to help train a constant supply of mentors in Year 10, with the departing Year 11 mentors training the new intake each year. In its first year, 12 at-risk Year 10 students were selected and given training aimed at building their confidence, speaking in public, running sessions to help younger children and first aid. In its second year, the number of mentors more than doubled to 26, with the original 12 involved in the new mentors' training. In its third year the scheme was given the Department for Education and Skills and National Mentoring Network Award for its work, with mentors' photographs displayed at a national British Red Cross exhibition in London called Face to Face. One of the mentors, aged 16, had been in trouble with the police 36 times in a year but after becoming one of its first mentors he became trouble free. 'Since I started volunteering my behaviour is much better. I'm proud of myself,' he said.

Peer research

Young people undertake activities such as surveys, interviews and questionnaires to explore issues that concern their peers and to seek solutions, for example, the 'Shared Learning in Action' approach (King and Occleston 1998) facilitated participation according to young people's own agendas.

Case Study 7

Peer research leading to face to face peer support at Wolstanton High School, Newcastle under Lyme, Staffordshire (Cartwright 2005)

In 2000 the peer support service BULLYinc was introduced at the school to make bonds between younger and older students in the school. It grew out of the peer supporters' own personal experiences and wanting to help others. After surveying the whole school student population of 832 students, the students discovered that 65 per cent of them felt bullying to be an important issue. This led to a review of the anti-bullying policy to be overseen by a working party of 20 teaching and non-teaching staff and a number of new anti-bullying strategies including peer support. Netta Cartwright trained the first two cohorts in 2002 and 2003 and the RC-trained co-ordinator continued the training subsequently. The buddies in 2005 explained to the author that:

'Once trained, we will be working with new buddies on a Wednesday morning in our weekly form sessions to introduce them to the duties they will acquire through being a buddy. We also hope that this time will give them an opportunity to gain confidence. Once the new buddies have been chosen we will inform the younger year groups in the school that there are still buddies to talk to. We continue to operate our drop-in centre services at dinnertime and will advise the next year group to do the same. We will tell the Year 10 buddies all of our ideas in the hope that they will take them on board and adapt them to suit their abilities and the students needs.'

Peer tutoring

Peer workers tutor others the same age or younger in reading, writing, thinking, spelling, maths and other academic skills. It is sometimes referred to as peer assisted learning (PAL) and can be particularly useful where the peer tutor is only a bit more advanced academically so both tutor and tutee benefit. Older students helping younger ones can be very beneficial for students with behavioural problems.

Case Study 8

St Marylebone School for Girls: one-to-one peer tutoring (Scherer-Thompson 2002)

Included in a range of peer support interventions in this school was a paired reading project where a sixth former was paired with a younger student who has been identified as needing extra support. The peer tutor met with the tutee on a regular basis in a specified room for 10–15 minutes where they worked on reading, pronunciation and comprehension of written material.

Peer support websites and email services

Websites are a means of publicizing and complementing existing peer support systems. They usually include the opportunity for those students too nervous for face to face contact to write for help by email. Schools keen to provide a fully inclusive service use email contact to provide one-to-one support anonymously. Some schools (as in the case study on the opposite page) used an email service as their first step in peer support.

Case Study 9

Email peer support at St Paul's School, London (Cowie and Hutson, 2005)

After an incidence of bullying, this all-boys school wanted to involve its students in decision making. Senior staff ran focus groups for all Year 9 boys to identify gaps in the pastoral system. The students requested an email peer support service to provide anonymous and confidential help for any boys seeking counselling. They felt that an email helpdesk would provide students with 'an open space to meet, without preconceptions, personalities or boundaries'. Eighty-two volunteers were reduced to a committed 25 for RC training with Netta Cartwright. After this, mixed age group teams of four worked together on a rota to respond to emails three times a week. The supervising teacher mediated the email process to ensure anonymity and have control over serious cases. She logged incoming emails sent by boys from their school email accounts. Then she cut and pasted them to a blank page and forwarded them to the team. They responded via the teacher who sent the replies back to the boys' email addresses. So far the scheme has been successful and has encouraged a more emotionally literate ethos in the school.

Student-led peer support as a model for increased student participation and citizenship

Most programmes as exemplified in the case studies are currently peer supporters delivering projects that have been planned by adults. They can potentially become peer-led projects controlled and planned primarily by the young people themselves and some are developing in this way. Participation and empowerment are issues central to the practice of peer support especially if it is introduced as part of the promotion of active citizenship (see Appendix 2).

Peer support provides opportunities for empowering both young people and adults and increasingly young people are able to influence local and national policy and events. This takes participation beyond mere tokenism and towards a more genuine participation where there are child initiated, shared decisions with adults. The Peer Support Forum had a young people's advisory group, which guided the work of the organization and as the newly formed Peer Support Network encourages young people to contribute to meetings and the website. By adapting this approach, schools could bring about a shift in the balance of power and the division of labour with young people having more responsibilities within schools.

The most essential point for adults to grasp is that peer support is about trust and taking risks by sharing with or delegating power to young people. This can be difficult for many adults, especially those who are feeling threatened within the education system. Research shows that teachers are less likely to emphasize empowerment than youth workers are (Shiner 2000) and peer support projects can challenge adult co-ordinators. This was not the case in most of the schools where staff were trained in the RC model, which emphasizes the empowerment of young people. The co-ordinator at Wolstanton High School, Clint Lakin, (case study 7) had completed a full RC course and continued to encourage students to take charge of their peer support service.

Young people may want to direct their project forward differently to how the teacher planned it and other teachers may fear this will set a precedent, undermining their authority – which often feels fragile. For schools to move towards more student-led peer support, perhaps staff can learn from the student model and develop their own peer support on similar lines. Staff and teacher support groups have already been set up in some schools in the West Midlands as a means to support staff in their teaching of students with special needs (Creese et al. 2000). Perhaps both staff and students each having access to their own peer support services could be a mutually beneficial step towards the promotion of a more supportive atmosphere in a school. Meaningful peer support cannot happen in isolation from the rest of the school. There must be the full backing of all members of the school community for it to grow and develop.

Chapter 3

Theories and research evidence on peer support projects in schools

 It is important to note that peer support isn't something that either exists or doesn't exist in a school.

(Moldrich and Carpentieri 2005)

Theories

There is a difference between school students helping each other in an everyday informal manner and a formal organized peer support structure. The former happens anyway but tends to be unreliable. Some students find the decision to seek help very difficult, and for many it is viewed as an admission of failure in their own and others' eyes (Le Surf and Lynch, 1999). Sharp, et al. (1994) found pupils wanted to be actively involved in offering support to their peers, and believed they had much to offer. However, Sharp and Cowie (1998) argue that research suggests schoolchildren and young people can be prevented from offering support by negative peer pressure and by doubts about the adequacy of that help. Formal programmes are established specifically to facilitate peer support happening more easily, reliably and effectively. Often there are wider aims in formal peer support and research indicates that it has a positive impact on:

- bullying behaviour;
- academic results;
- division of labour;
- the student voice;
- student/teacher relationships.

The fundamental theory underpinning peer support, especially those offering emotional support, is that human beings are essentially altruistic and therefore the practice of peers supporting each other is part of human nature. Cowie and Sharp (1996) refer to arguments that 'humans have a strong born motivation to form co-operative, supportive relationships with one another'. They argue that programmes of peer support are only a structured extension of 'the natural willingness of young people to act in co-operative, friendly ways towards one another'. Young people's eager willingness to help each other is indeed testified by Moldrich and Carpentieri's (2005) analysis of their call statistics, revealing that concern for other young people is the fourth most common reason children call their helpline. 'Hundreds of thousands' of young people have told them over the last 20 years that children are far more likely to ask their peers for help rather than an adult, especially in the early stages of a problem before it reaches crisis point. Sometimes peers work together co-operatively as a survival tactic to keep each other out of danger. Young people form gangs with their friends to help them stay safe and keep out of trouble, according to research carried out among young people in four deprived areas of west Scotland (Hill 2006). The study showed that young people shared knowledge about which areas and people to avoid and deployed certain strategies to avoid trouble. It also challenges over-simple assumptions that areas of deprivation have a negative culture of parenting and that peer group activity is largely antisocial.

There are a number of theories to account for the altruistic motivations and co-operative activities of peer supporters. Cowie and Sharp (1996) in their survey observe that animal studies 'suggest that primates possess powerful mechanisms of reassurance and reconciliation that allow them to cope with the socially negative effects of aggression within their own social group'. They cite psychodynamic, attachment and family systems theories and research into siblings, conflict, co-operation and peer relationships as illuminating current thinking on why peer support works.

Rowan (1976) places the origin of organized peer support within the theoretical framework of humanistic psychology and gives an account of RC as an example of a type of peer support. This is the co-counselling model used in the first school to have peer support in the UK (see Chapter 1) and in some of the other case studies. RC (Jackins 1965) is a theory with the concept of peer support practice leading to systemic change (see Chapter 1). This accords with Vygotsky's idea of creating psychology for social purposes and as a tool for social change rather than just a mirror of reality (Daniels 1996). RC is a therapy that has developed into a peer self-help movement and has a number of social implications (Scheff 1972). The theoretical framework for its practice has similarities with the concepts and methods of other models of counselling and psychotherapy such as Rogers (1957) and others cited in Somers (1972) where he discusses these similarities. He describes RC therapy as having a working assumption that all human beings have a core being which is loving, zestful, co-operative, curious and communicative, and a creative and flexible intelligence. These assumptions are more specific than those of the humanistic group but many therapists work with at least some of them. The relevance of these ideas to peer support is that Jackins, Rogers and others maintain that the helper's experiencing of her own core being is a critical part of her ability to help her client and believe in the client's underlying core being. This is seen as preferable to the helper maintaining an aware intellectual belief in her client at the sacrifice of her own emotional well-being. The RC theory postulates a socio-historical cause for people's distressed behaviour patterns, which leads them away from their core being (Jackins 1965). The focus of the therapy is the discharge or release of feelings, which is in effect similar to Rogers' sixth or breakthrough stage. The difference is that for Rogers and others the release of emotions is merely a by-product or part of the process of therapy but for Jackins it is the main aim. Another major difference as pointed out by Rowan is in the treatment of self-denigration. Whereas the Rogerian approach sees self-rejection as necessary for authentic growth Jackins views putting oneself down as a distress that has been reinforced down the years by parents, teachers, peers and others. This emphasis of the counsellor on seeing the client in a positive and realistic manner, always aware that any negative aspects are part of undischarged distress patterns, is the RC model used when training people to become peer supporters. By learning co-counselling they are able to swap attention as client and counsellor and support each other in their work as peer supporters as well as offering one way attention to other students. As Rowan remarks 'co-counselling uses up a lot of Kleenex!'

These kind of humanistic ideas are a departure from Freud, who created psychoanalysis and other traditional psychological theories. Freud recognized that people who talked to an attentive listener could be released from the effects of earlier traumas or mishaps in life and used catharsis under hypnosis to get to the roots of a problem. However, psychoanalysis has the assumption that human antisocial and destructive behaviour is intrinsic and therefore inevitable. The humanistic theories view this behaviour as learned. Cowie and Sharp (1996) point out that if children are brought up in an excessively violent, uncaring environment where personal rights are not valued they will adapt a defensive stance that not only retards their curiosity and imagination, but also develops remorseless behaviour that is unsociable, survivalist and exploitative of others. Cowie and Sharp (1996) discuss the role of peer relationships in children's development. If peer relationships are good with conflicts being coped with successfully they will be well prepared for successful relationships in later life. If they are bad there could be long-term problems. Cowie et al. (1994) consider two main aspects of social relationships – affiliation and power. Children who are neglected or rejected by their peers will suffer interpersonal difficulties in adulthood. Within social groups power relationships are inevitable, as some people are more likely to become leaders because of greater physical, intellectual, emotional or financial strength. When that power is abused this causes distress to others, which is central to bullying behaviour and the damage caused to individuals and school communities. Peer support by promoting co-operation, social responsibility, friendship and conflict resolution enables young people to prevent, overcome and transcend the damage caused by antisocial and distressed behaviour.

This is not the place to fully consider complex theories when looking at the impact of peer support on system reform. Rigorous scientific research of outcomes and processes of peer support interventions is difficult to achieve. That kind of empirical evidence requires a control group, with directly comparable features between projects and precise definitions of variables. A time frame enabling longer term outcomes to be evaluated is also necessary. Measuring peer support is also problematic bearing in mind the many interpretations of 'success' and that it is an activity that needs more than quantitative methods. Claimed outcomes such as changes in school ethos, bullying incidences, levels of social responsibility and any effects from adding teacher peer support teams are inevitably coloured by the assumptions and values of the evaluators and the systems they work in.

Nevertheless, the next section will survey the evidence so far.

Research evidence

There is a growing body of literature which explores the ways in which peer support schemes in schools contribute towards strategies to combat bullying and racial harassment, as well as helping children deal with stresses at home and in school. Research shows that peer support can encourage a more caring atmosphere in schools and promote greater democracy; a less stressful ethos; and a shift in power towards young people. Schools with these kinds of values are also more able to set up and sustain peer support (Carr 1994). The Keele Anti-bullying Project (Glover and Cartwright 1998) looked at the different impacts of peer support depending on the type of atmosphere in schools, and found that those schools with the more caring and democratic values were more conducive to the approach than those which were more authoritarian in approach.

Examples of research on peer support in general, with comprehensive evaluations of large projects revealing a number of successful features, are Cowie and Wallace (2000), Naylor and Cowie (1999) and Carr (1988). Small scale and qualitative evaluations have also provided evidence of positive results from a variety of peer work interventions over the last two decades, both in the UK and elsewhere. Examples of research on more specific forms of peer support are: befriending (Konet 1991); peer tutoring (Franca et al. 1990); peer-delivered health promotion (Clements and Buczkiewicz 1993); peer mentoring and peer mediation (Stacey 1996); bereavement support (Quarmby 1993); group counselling (Sprinthall et al. 1992); telephone counselling (Boehm et al 1991); Conflict resolution (Lane et al 1992); Circle of Friends approach (Newton et al. 1996); the impact of peer listening and counselling (Cowie and Sharp 1996 and Rogers et al. 1999); and improved behaviour from previously challenging pupils (Lowenstein 1989).

This research shows a number of common outcomes with three main beneficiaries: the young people who receive peer support, the peer supporters and the school. The main benefits are listed below with some examples of researchers:

- Increased confidence and self-esteem for both peer supporters and their clients (Hahn and LeCapitaine 1990).
- Improved communication and social skills for peer supporters: (Cowie et al. 2002, Christopher et al. 1991, CAPP 1998).
- A better atmosphere in school and the wider community (Naylor and Cowie 1999, CAPP 1998).
- Improved behaviour and a reduction in bullying (Lowenstein 1989, Smith and Sharp 1994, Baginsky 2001).
- Peer support projects enhance supportive pastoral systems (Glover and Cartwright 1998).
- Better academic performance (James et al. 1991, Simmons et al. 1995, CAPP 1998).
- Greater student involvement in problem solving (CAPP 1998).
- Positive impact on disabled students (McGee et al. 1992, Burley et al. 1994).
- Reduction in self-harm and substance abuse (CAPP 1998).
- Young people are more likely to seek help from peers than adults (Cowie et al. 2002, Le Surf and Lynch 1999).
- Pupil counsellors can offer unique perspectives on why their peers may be suffering and can often identify appropriate strategies for helping them (Carr 1988, Sharp et al. 1994).

- Young people report that a peer support system in their school is useful whether they used it or not (Cowie et al. 2002).
- Young people more tolerant of the behaviour of others (Mellanby et al. 2000)
- Increased practice of safe sex or less likely to be sexually active among certain groups (Mellanby et al. 2000).
- 16 year olds' increased knowledge of sex, contraception and sexually transmitted diseases (Mellanby et al. 2000).
- More acceptance of sex education by 16 year olds (Mellanby et al 2000)
- Young people less likely to believe that intercourse should be part of relationships for under 16s (Mellanby et al. 2000).
- Enhancing the National Curriculum (QCA 1999).
- Raising standards in the mainstream curriculum (Cowie and Sharp 1996).
- Peers can accurately assess each other (Stefani 1994).
- Peer support is cost-effective (Sharp et al. 1994).

Potential difficulties

Although there are many benefits to peer support, research has also identified some problems relating to the practice and setting up of such schemes. A major problem to be overcome is that young people do not always take advantage of the help on offer. A potential hurdle therefore is finding students who are confident enough to provide a service to challenge this and not be discouraged and disappointed when students do not readily take it up. Sharp and Cowie (1998) argue that research suggests schoolchildren want to help peers they perceive to be in distress, but can be held back by negative peer pressure and lack of confidence in the adequacy of their help.

Once peer supporters have been trained, establishing credibility with other students can be difficult. There is a danger of their being targeted, ridiculed and seen as 'geeks' (Naylor 1997). If the staff are not kept informed they may dismiss the whole project if they feel that peer supporters are trying to do the work of adult professional services. They could feel threatened or annoyed if some peer supporters become over involved. These problems are compounded if there are unclear boundaries about child protection and confidentiality. Inappropriate disclosures can cause distress to all involved. Even with the teachers who are part of the process there can be empowerment issues with conflicts between them and peer supporters when the power balance shifts.

Time management, lack of resources and lack of commitment from senior management are also a major challenge. Schools often find it hard after peer support has been set up to invest the resources needed for staff to supervise the peer supporters and keep the momentum going. Baginsky (2001) found this to be the case in 14 schools where the NSPCC were involved (see Chapter 8).

Inadequate training is another issue that can create more problems than solutions. Baginsky also found that training might be appropriate for stereotypical 'teenage' problems but it was inadequate and too short to prepare them for dealing with students with behavioural difficulties.

Other problems associated with peer support are as follows:

- Reduced confidence in peer supporters if inadequately trained and supported (Sharp and Cowie 1998).
- Frustration where raised hopes and expectations are not met (Baginsky 2001).
- Lack of adequate supervision (Lewis and Lewis 1996).
- Gender differences and imbalance (Storm 1991).
- Limited impact in reducing student violence (Cowie and Olafsson 2000).
- Psychological readiness is necessary to gain from peer counsellor experience (Silver et al. 1992).

Studies have shown more advantages than disadvantages to both peer supporters and their clients as well as to schools in general. Cowie and Hutson (2005) suggest that research so far points to success lying in 'a process of flexible monitoring and clear observation of the needs of potential users'. Also supervising teachers must take into account the social context and 'make use of the situated knowledge that the young peer supporters bring to their task'.

Stage 2
Peer support training

Chapter 4

Setting up programmes and training

 The secret of getting ahead is getting started. The secret of getting started is breaking your complex overwhelming tasks into small manageable tasks, and then starting on the first one.

(Mark Twain)

Programmes as part of the whole-school ethos

This chapter provides practical tips on how to set up peer support programmes and the training outlined in Chapters 5 to 7. As shown in Chapter 1 there is a myriad of types of peer support each with its own set of values, assumptions and processes with varieties of knowledge and skills used. Carr (1994) has identified over 30 different terms used to describe peer workers and there are countless projects in the United Kingdom alone. Connexions and Youth and Community Services are involved in numerous programmes and over 1,000 have been set up by Childline. The author alone has set up over 35 projects in the Midlands. A list of organizations setting up and or promoting peer support is in Appendix 3. What unites all these under the banner of 'peer support' is a set of core principles as outlined in Chapter 2.

Peer support programmes are all rooted in the idea of the peer as helper and based on the assumption that young people naturally wish to help each other. At the same time it is important to be alert to the diverse ways in which peer support systems can develop and to ensure equality of access so that certain children are not inadvertently excluded. Alongside the dynamic growth of the peer support movement is the increasing recognition that the process should be open and accessible to all students and not a selected few. As more diverse groups of young people become involved they themselves are increasing the range of activities and expanding the vision of peer support in the future.

It is important that stakeholders understand that peer support is about improving relationships for everybody in schools not just the students concerned. By engaging a wider set of community members it can help enhance a school's caring ethos. In particular the involvement of senior management and school governors can play a very positive role in setting up and sustaining peer support programmes. They can offer advice and encouragement as well as provide practical support and solutions to administrative problems. Peer support works best when its principles are embedded in the everyday workings of the school and there is a shared ownership and understanding of the key aspects of the programme. This position will take some time to establish though it can happen more quickly where a school already has an ethos of students taking responsibility for themselves; then it can be easier for peer support principles to be adopted throughout the school. However, experience shows that even in schools where there is no history of student participation it is possible to fulfil peer support principles and set up programmes.

Ideally before setting up a programme the whole school and senior management need to be on board, but if this is not the case it is possible to proceed and work towards their involvement during the process. However, it is essential to ensure there are resources to properly support an established peer support service and make it sustainable. Every programme will necessarily be designed and customized for each institution and there are detailed templates for programmes outlined in this chapter. It may help, however, to provide an overview of the key stages in setting up peer support. This can then be adapted to local contexts.

The first steps

Needs analysis

Cowie and Wallace (2000) identify the starting point of peer support as 'an awareness of need and the desire to find a way to meet that need'. They suggest the conducting of a needs analysis before designing and setting up a programme. This involves identifying the needs of the school at that time and assessing the resources available before moving to an intervention. Their book devotes a whole chapter to this with examples of needs analyses. Childline (2002) also conducts a needs analysis before starting work in their schools.

A needs analysis can be kept simple or can be quite detailed depending on the time and resources that are available. Some examples of the kind of questions that might be addressed in such an exercise include:

Needs analysis basic questions:
- What is the school's understanding of peer support and why does it want to introduce a scheme?
- What resources are available and what will it cost in time, finance and staff commitment?
- Are there target groups as users and providers of peer support?
- What are the aims of the scheme?
- What model will be adopted, for example, befriending, mentoring, counselling-based, mediation, conflict resolution, circle time?
- How will it fit the school's culture?

- Is support and commitment guaranteed from senior staff, governors and all sections of the school community?
- Are students used to being consulted on school issues?
- What is the time span to be worked to?
- What are the ethical issues and how can safety checks be put in place?
- Will all new staff be introduced to the scheme during induction?
- Which member/s of staff will take responsibility for running the scheme?
- How will peer supporters be selected so they reflect the student body, particularly in relation to gender and ethnicity?
- What will be the role of peer supporters and what are the boundaries of this role?
- How can confidentiality (including child protection issues) be made explicit, and covered in training and supervision?
- Will the selection, training and implementation of the scheme be sensitive to the backgrounds of the students?
- Who will provide the skilled, experienced and appropriate training necessary?
- Where will the service be located and will it be suitable and accessible?
- Who will assist, supervise and support the peer supporters?
- How will the scheme be monitored and evaluated?
- How will the scheme be publicized?
- How will staff and students stay motivated?

Appointing a co-ordinator(s) or key worker(s)

This is another early step in preparing for the project. Co-ordinators can be drawn from staff (preferably senior management) or outside agencies. Often they are school counsellors or youth workers. Sometimes special educational needs co-ordinators (SENCOs) or learning support assistants (LSAs) are appointed. The person(s) needs to be motivated and committed with enough non-contact time for the necessary administrative work. Enough time needs to be allowed for this aspect of the role. Day-to-day tasks include: drawing up contracts, writing memos, producing rotas and sending out reminders for the peer supporters. The key worker will often need to work on his or her own and be adaptable. It helps if they have had suitable training and are not landed with the job by default or thrust into it without consultation.

The key worker could lead a steering team with between two and twelve representatives from the school, community and outside agencies. The team could support the co-ordinator in building an infrastructure for the programme and preparing for the project could include the needs analysis above. The team may no longer be needed once the early stages are over and the service is established. Responsibilities of the co-ordinator and the team if there is one could include:

- *Building on and consolidating existing practices.* The project could develop from a prefect system already in place or existing situations such as students' concerns about bullying, an individual crisis or a school policy that is not working.

- *Evaluating the need for a particular type of peer support.* The team could organize surveys, questionnaires and/or interviews, refer to inspection reports and research schemes elsewhere (see Appendices 1 and 2). From this a proposal clarifying aims and objectives can be made that suits the institution's needs. For example, a school with a school counsellor would be in a good position to set up peer counselling whereas a school with a strong special needs department may wish to develop peer education.

- *Consulting the whole school*. The proposal should include the background research, the aims and objectives, the design and expected costs, time schedule and resource implications. This can be discussed with governors, staff, students and parents/carers or at least their representatives. It is important to allow time for approval to be confirmed so the project can proceed with the full commitment and support from governors and senior management.

- *Establishing funding*. Ideally finance should be secured for at least two years for the project to start up. Depending on the size and nature of the project, costs can include: extra salary for the co-ordinator, trainer's fees, room hire, supply cover for staff training, administration, publicity, books, videos and other materials. Many institutions finance projects from their own budgets and this kind of commitment motivates the sustaining of the project. However, local and national charities such as Barclays New Futures are often good sources of income. The Standards Funds, Connexions, The Children Fund and the Healthy Schools Initiative are also potential funders. It is worth approaching some external agencies that may be willing to provide free training.

Peer supporters' drop-in room

- *Securing other resources*. Time resources, suitable facilities and accommodation will need to be arranged for the training of personnel and operation of the service. A regular base is needed for some projects such as peer listening, mediation or mentoring. Preferably the space or room is not shared with adults and clear guidelines need to be in place to ensure it is not misused.

- *Planning a timescale of action*. A schedule planned in some detail for at least one academic year but usually two or three ahead is necessary. The timing of events will depend largely on the academic calendar of the peer supporters' year group. Training sessions for students could be during personal social and health education (PSHE) time, on staff training days, residentials or on different school days over a period of time. If the service is part of a GNVQ Health and Social Care course, training can take place in curriculum time. Although many schools run courses at lunchtimes, twilight time or at weekends this is not recommended as it undermines the importance of the activity and can exclude many students as well as exploiting the goodwill of staff. Having a timescale will ensure the support of senior management and governors and can form the basis of bids for finance from outside agencies.

- *Deciding on student personnel*. Most institutions opt to train students from the penultimate cohort or the one before so that there is at least two years for them to work as peer supporters before they leave. Many secondary schools train some of their Year 9 or Year 10 students and have a rolling programme. In the primary schools usually Year 4 and/or Year 5 students are trained. In some schools their Year 11 and 12 students are trained but this is becoming less popular with the increasing demands on post-16 students.

- *Appointing staff supervisors and, if necessary, specialist support*. The latter will be needed if the project requires specialist knowledge such as sex or drugs education. In this case students need to be constantly updated and be clear about the boundaries of their competence and know when to refer users on to their supervisors. All projects must have regular (rather than ad hoc) adult supervision otherwise peer supporters will be isolated and lose enthusiasm and momentum. Supervisors monitor the service and provide guidance and support to the peer supporters. They are also points of referral when peer supporters are taken beyond the limits of competency.

- *Deciding on the target groups for support*. This depends on the type of project. For example a peer listening service could be available to all students and may also be proactively targeted at Year 7. A peer education service may target students with reading difficulties. Consultation with the pastoral and departmental headteachers will be necessary at this stage to discuss the logistics and agree on methods of service delivery.

- *Appointing trainer/s*. They must be qualified in the listening and counselling skills to be taught and in experiential learning techniques. Experience in training young people is highly beneficial. Negotiating the time, length and content of training sessions will be necessary and perhaps some initial training of staff before the student training takes place. See Appendix 3 for orgainzations that can help.

Next steps: preparing for training

The next major step is preparing the student training. Ideally staff supervisors are trained in the same model as the students. They can be trained beforehand or learn alongside the students. In both cases they would assist the trainer in student training and eventually train future cohorts in-house to sustain the programme. The content of the supervisors' training will be similar to the students' course with the addition of referral procedures and how to supervise the peer supporters and administrate the project. Length of courses depends on the existing skills of the staff but ideally six to twelve hours is needed for their training.

The key steps in setting up the training are:

- *Advertising the training course*. Posters, assemblies, notices in school newsletters and other publicity to inform all students in the targeted year group(s) need to be in place at least a month before the course is due to begin.

- **Recruiting trainees.** How this is done and who is recruited is a crucial stage of the project and will determine its nature, scope and success. Some institutions use formal selection with application forms and interviews. Others use positive selection with peer and/or adult nominations to ensure a balance of gender, race and physical academic ability. Both approaches have their advantages and ideally a combination of the two is the most successful. Cowie et al. (2002) describe some issues with the recruitment and retention of boys and young men as peer supporters and offers some possible solutions to this including thinking creatively about the training on offer and the types of peer support activities. The paper explores how schools have worked to minimize the stigma of accessing peer support. Self-selection can be useful in the context of self-help around particular issues such as bereavement or bullying. A few institutions train as many students as possible, for example Millennium Youth Volunteers are selected after whole cohorts have been trained and small primary schools train whole year groups. The Peer Support Forum have published a manual with proformas of posters, application forms, interview questions, letters of refusal and acceptance, and parental consent forms (Scherer-Thompson 2002).

- **Creating support roles for students not selected for training.** Inherent in the values of peer support is the belief that no student is unsuitable. However, for those students who have applied but would find the peer support role difficult other roles in the service can be offered. For example they could be receptionists in a peer listening service, peer artists, researchers or website designers. It is also important to explain to an applicant with sensitivity and clarity why s/he has not been selected for a training course.

- **Arranging venues and consulting with staff on the schedule.** Busy staff need to be reminded and consulted again on the best times for training during the school calendar and which rooms can be used. The training environment must be comfortable and spacious to enable small group-work and to show students they are valued.

- **Preparing the students for training.** About two weeks before the training the co-ordinator will need to send information to them and their parents regarding the type of training, dates, times and venues. Emphasize the commitment required and the necessity to attend all the sessions. Remind them to inform teachers if they are to miss lessons and to negotiate how they can catch up on their work. If they are to be assessed ensure they know how it will be done. Ask parents to sign permission slips. Parents may refuse permission even when their children want to do it. The usual reasons are anxieties about their children missing lessons and the time commitment to the project afterwards. Occasionally they will be concerned about the content of the training and the responsibilities their children will be taking on. The best way to deal with these concerns is to provide full information about the training, the project and the level of staff support that will be available for the peer supporters.

- **Training the selected students.** To successfully train more than 10 students two trainers or if not possible a trainer and at least one assistant from the school staff (the key worker(s)) is necessary. Courses vary from a few hours to several days or more depending on the content. Some sessions may be just short introductions to the ideas for peer support but they will need to be followed up with longer, in-depth courses if peer support is to be established. Ongoing training and supervision is especially useful in maintaining a successful project. Quality training and materials is essential for the core skills required for all peer support programmes.

Students on a training course

Core peer support skills explored in training

basic counselling and listening

communication

body language

recognizing and dealing with emotions

safety

empathy

confidentiality

boundaries

child protection and referral

- *Specific skill training* will be necessary, in addition, to fit the type of service to be provided, for example mediation skills. Interactive and experiential training works best with young people, preferably games interspersed with short activities. This is especially true with primary students. Some trainers use role play, photographs and everyday scenarios for students to practise skills. Others prefer them to use real situations from their own lives or a combination of both. Some courses are for the students only though experience shows that by having staff supervisor(s) present in at least some of the sessions can help them bond with the group, experience the same model and train to teach it themselves. See Chapters 5 to 7 for examples of a variety of training models.

- *Assessing students*. The recruitment process is the first point of assessment. Further assessments of a student's ability to be a peer supporter can be made during and after the training. A self-evaluation before the training may help students recognize whether they can peer support or whether they would prefer a different role. (See Chapter 10 for more details.)

- *Accreditation*. Some schools accredit courses so that students have recognized certification and these have their own assessment criteria (see Chapter 9).

- *Evaluation of the course and assessment of learning*. Questionnaires for students and staff to fill in at the end of the session will help in assessing how skilled the participants feel and provide pointers for changes in future courses (see Appendix 4 and Scherer-Thompson 2002 for examples). If you wish to find out attitude changes in participants, a before and after questionnaire is useful (see Appendix 4 and Cowie and Sharp, 1996, pages 140–141 for useful questions).

- *Record keeping, evaluating and monitoring the service*. These overlapping but separate processes provide evidence of the benefits of the service, gain credibility, help secure future funding, address any concerns and give participants and users an opportunity to reflect on their experiences. They are necessary for reviewing the outcomes and processes of the service from a variety of perspectives and developing it further. The simplest way is to design a system where data is collected and collated systematically (see Chapter 9).

The training course

The purpose of the training is generally twofold: promoting the personal development of the peer supporters themselves, and training them in specific skills to support others. When devising any course it is important to ensure a balance between the two. Ideally this should be continually reviewed with the participants before and during the training.

Key features

The following aspects are important when planning training courses:

- Training should have a clear structure allowing for flexibility.
- Training should be interactive, participative and learner centred.
- The atmosphere should be informal, creative, lively, playful, constructive and thoughtful.
- An ambience of trust and confidentiality is essential.
- Training materials need to reflect an inclusive society and be pitched at the right level of age and ability.
- Careful timing of sessions should ensure breaks where informal bonding and idea sharing can take place.
- A variety of training techniques should be used to maintain momentum and interest.
- Time needs to be built in for students to reflect on the training and what they are learning.
- A clear brief needs to be drawn up for the trainer(s).

The trainer(s)

The success of any programme relies heavily on the role of the trainers/facilitators. These roles need to be carefully allocated to ensure maximum benefit from experienced trainers and those novice teachers and school students who they train to teach peer support courses. Programmes can use a wide range of trainers including:

- LEA staff.
- Freelance trainers, usually specializing in issues connected to the peer support programme such as health, substance abuse, conflict resolution, counselling or sex education.
- Youth and community workers.
- Teachers.
- Health promotion staff linked to the school.

- Trainers from charities, organizations and training agencies specialising in peer support training such as NSPCC, CHIPS, The Mental Health Foundation, LEAP, The Quaker Foundation, Peer Support Works and Co-counselling International (see Appendix 4).

There is no blueprint for the best facilitator and all the above can do an excellent job provided they have a clear brief which they are capable of undertaking and are allowed the necessary resources. Teachers may find knowing the students in a different context may help or hinder the process. Experience shows however that they are just as likely to have good results as external facilitators. Whether the trainer/s are internal or external it is useful to ensure that they:

- Meet the group before the training sessions if possible.
- Produce a detailed training outline clearly reflecting the school's brief.
- Do not communicate inappropriate personal views or moral judgements during training.
- Reflect the school's equal opportunities and inclusion policies.
- Have a good rapport with young people and an understanding of their issues.

The training will be somewhat different to the usual school lessons because of the co-operative, collaborative and confidential style necessary for students to work as a team .

Confidentiality and referrals

Confidentiality is a necessary ground rule in any training which aims to provide an atmosphere of trust and co-operation. The trainer will need to explain the rules of confidentiality within the bounds of the Children Act 1989 and ensure participants understand and give informed consent. Although it is fine for participants to describe and explain the processes learned on the course to other people, strict confidentiality about what people say about themselves or others is essential. This means nothing said or done in the course is repeated to anyone and is also not referred to again to the persons who said or did it unless they refer to it themselves. However, should any serious disclosure (for example, sexual abuse) be made to the student or adults they would be bound to refer the matter to a senior member of staff. In turn, peer helpers must make this clear at the onset with any students to whom they offer support or counselling (see Chapter 9). They must also understand the importance of keeping dramatic information confidential and that matters spoken about in a peer support session must not become playground gossip.

Abuse is legally defined under the criteria of sexual, physical, emotional and neglect. The Children Act 1989 and 2004 states that if a person under 17 years old discloses an abuser, action should be taken. This means informing participants that if any serious disclosure is made to a trainee peer helper or trainer the latter would be bound by the Children Act to refer on the material to the teacher in charge of child protection in the organization.

Techniques and activities

Techniques will vary depending on the objectives of the course and trainers need to understand the reasons for including any activity, know how it can contribute to learning objectives and ensure it is used appropriately. Many of the following techniques and activities involve the development of key skills and any one activity can contribute to a number of learning objectives. Several are referred to in the programmes outlined in Chapters 5 to 7.

● *Active listening – 15 minutes*
  Go over each 'do' and 'don't'

DO	DON'T
be respectful	be overbearing or probing
be delighted	be disapproving or uninterested
be thinking	be mechanical or routine
be caring and interested	be sentimental or brusque
be encouraging and accepting	be judgemental or too sympathetic
be confident	be hesitant, worried or apologetic
encourage discharge of emotions	give advice or slick answers

Explain how our natural ability to discharge emotions aids the healing process and enables people to think more clearly after confusing feelings have been released. People find it hard to act on advice if they have unreleased emotions and have not thought of their own solutions. Laughing, raging, crying, shaking, blushing, yawning and talking are all important to discharge and heal the distresses caused by anger, grief, fear, embarrassment, nervousness, boredom and other negative feelings. Other active listening skills are verbal and non-verbal as follows:

Acknowledging: '*I understand*' , '*I see*', '*OK*', '*That sounds really important to you*', *nodding, eye contact, open body language.*

Checking: '*You seem to be angry*', '*Am I right in thinking you said...*'

Clarification: '*I'm not sure I understand. Did you say...?*', '*Did this happen three times or did you say twice?*'

Affirmation: '*Thank you for coming*', '*You have given me a lot of information, thank you*'.

Empathy: '*I can understand why you are worried about this*', '*I think this situation has been very difficult for you and you're getting impatient.*'

Asking a variety of questions: '*Could you tell me more about this please?*', '*When exactly did that happen?*', '*Who else have you spoken to about this?*'

Reflecting: *(John says, '*I'm fed up with all this*'). '*You are fed up? What particularly upsets you?*'

Summarizing: '*So there seems to be several things that are important to you....*', '*It started off with one incident and then there were two more over the next week*'.

Also important are:
Timing: Questions and comments should be at a pace the speaker can deal with.

Tone of voice and volume: The listener may sometimes need to vary tone and volume. If you need to move from soft to firmer tone or from soft to louder volume, it is best to do it in stages. Sudden switches can disturb speakers.

● *Appreciations on backs*. Participants, including the trainer, each write their names on a piece of A4 with a small symbol of themselves at the top. They get it pinned on their back by another person. Then they go around the whole group writing what they like about each person on the sheet pinned to their backs. When finished everyone sits in a circle and reads out one of their appreciations and says it is true. If time permits they can read out all their appreciations to the group and say they are all true especially the one that says...(their favourite one).

Students writing appreciations

● *Case studies* are written scenarios for analysis and problem solving. The group practises these skills by identifying key issues and action strategies. As well as providing practical applications of participants' ideas in virtually real-life situations, case studies develop team-working and communication skills.

● *Character-circle* is a role-play activity where one person in role, possibly the trainer, sits in the centre and each participant has a role (such as mother, sister, friend) who relates to the person in the middle. They all then role-play around a situation that the central character is involved in.

● *Co-counselling* is two co-counsellors taking turns in the roles of counsellor (listener) and client (person being listened to). They swap roles so each person has equal time to counsel and be listened to. This involves both thinking about the client's needs and concerns with a view to resolving the client's feelings and practical problems. The counsellor's task is to give the client the opportunity to explore and clarify his/her situation so he/she can live more resourcefully and have greater well-being. The counsellor's job is to enable a client to think about her/himself, life, relationships and situations. The counsellor should never discount the client's own thinking and should avoid giving advice. The counsellor is to help her/his clients to discharge or release feelings in the counselling session so they can think more clearly to find solutions for themselves and be able to have more control over emotions in their everyday life.

● *Co-counselling mini sessions* is short periods of time (one to fifteen minutes each) where two people take turns co-counselling. This can be on any topic that is keeping their minds occupied at that time (this is helpful when people have just come in from other activities or travelling) or on a specific question, such as 'what is good and new in your life?' 'What is your goal for this activity?' and 'How has your life been affected by the activity?'. Mini sessions can also be used to give participants a chance to let out their feelings after having listened to something for a while. They may need a short break or there may be emotional reactions to process, for example after someone told their story in front of the group.

- *Coloured ribbons*. Have a collection of sets of two ribbons the same colour such as two red ribbons, two purple and two yellow. Give one ribbon out to each participant so they can find a person with the same colour ribbon to be their partner in an activity.

- *Confidentiality* means no one refers to what a person has said or done to anyone outside or inside the room. This is because people may not want to be reminded of what they have said or done or they may not want to be identified by it. Keeping to this confidentiality greatly improves the safety in any group and will allow people to share more of their emotions and thoughts.

- *Demonstrations of counselling* are when someone is counselled in front of the group to show a particular technique of counselling or allow someone to tell their particular story. It's important that the person agrees to do this and that it is fairly short. The person in front of the group also needs to be allowed to go as deeply into their feelings as they want to. It is important that the rules of confidentiality above have been set up clearly with the group.

- *Drawings, pictures, photographs and cartoons*. These can be ready-made or created by participants individually or as a group. Discussions on ready-made images help to clarify feelings and ideas around specific issues. Individual and group images with words and labels added can reveal beliefs and illustrate attitudes to form the basis for discussions. Collaborative poster designs promote many thinking and communication skills.

- *Fast forward* and *action replay* are drama activities developing the character role play further when characters and dialogue are established. With the former the trainer stops the interaction at any point to change it by introducing a new angle. The latter activity enables a scene to be replayed with the role players behaving differently with different attitudes.

- *Freeze-frame* is a technique in role play where participants in role stop and describe how they are feeling and the rest of the group is asked how they feel and what should happen next.

- *Games* and *drama activities* are essential for energizing participants, helping them to relax and introducing topics. They can be a practical application of concepts and information and range from simple card games to complex board games as well as physical activities. They are also examples of techniques participants can use as peer supporters when working with other students. It is crucial that games are designed to be inclusive for participants of all physical and learning abilities within the group. See the next section (page 48) for examples of games.

- *Ground rules* should be drawn up by the group at the start with guidance from the trainer. Group ownership of the rules enables easier handling of behaviour that contravenes them. On a flip chart or whiteboard write their suggestions until the whole group agrees to them. Put these up in every training session and refer to them if anyone breaks them. Ensure that confidentiality is included and explain it (see above). Also include respect, explaining that participants must listen to and respect each others' viewpoints. Any disagreements must be expressed and met constructively with no personal criticism.

Examples of ground rules:

1. Listen to others.
2. Let everyone have a turn.
3. Keep confidentiality.
4. No threatening behaviour.
5. No physical violence.
6. No making fun of anyone.
7. No put-downs.

- *Hot seating* is where one of the participants answers in role the questions put to them by the others.
- *Introductions* are helpful for the group to bond and begin trusting each other. Participants take turns to talk briefly about themselves with support from the trainer.
- *Life line* is an exercise where each participant draws a path-line in the form of a river, road or tree to represent their life story, writing and drawing significant events along the path, possibly with comments.

LIFELINE (River of Life)

Name: *Mandy Richards*   Date: *24 April 2006*

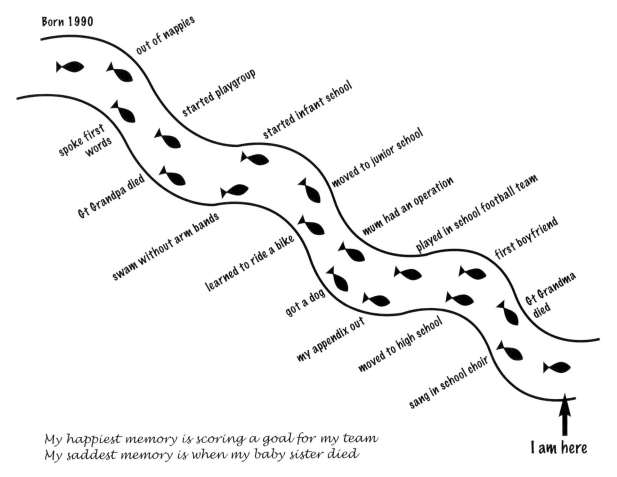

Born 1990

out of nappies

started playgroup

started infant school

moved to junior school

spoke first words

Gt Grandpa died

swam without arm bands

learned to ride a bike

got a dog

my appendix out

moved to high school

mum had an operation

played in school football team

first boyfriend

Gt Grandma died

sang in school choir

I am here

My happiest memory is scoring a goal for my team
My saddest memory is when my baby sister died

- *Opening* and *closing circles*. Opening circles provide the chance for participants to quickly get to know each others' names and to begin in a positive manner. They stand or sit in a circle and take turns to say names and something good and/or new they have experienced recently. Closing circles provide a chance to reflect on the day's training and finish in an upbeat manner. For example they could each say a highlight and something they like about the trainer's delivery and, time permitting, appreciate something about the person on their left.

- *Panels*. A group of 3–5 young people are chosen for their particular identities or stories to form a panel sitting together in a row in front of the group. They are asked the same set of questions by the facilitator, trainer or counsellor who is sitting close by. The questions are usually related to identities: what is good about having a certain identity (such as a girl, a boy, Asian, white, young, school student and so on)? What is difficult? What do you never want to hear again about people with your identity? This gives young people the chance to speak about their identity and to receive attention from the group. It also gives an opportunity for others who do not share the identity to learn about this group. After a panel it is useful to have mini sessions so students can express the emotions they felt during the panel. It is all right if they start to show emotion during the panel providing it does not disrupt it.

- *Quick-thinking* is where participants call out ideas on a topic to stimulate creative thinking for open-ended task oriented projects. For example a group may be asked to think laterally about an issue such as why do young people bully others? It is very effective when small groups make presentations of their findings to the whole group.

- *Relationship counselling* is a process whereby one person counsels two people who wish to improve their relationship. A couple may wish to improve an already good relationship or they may have a dispute or problem between them that they would like to sort out. Another disputing pair may not like each other and would like to work out how they can live alongside each other in their school or workplace without causing each other problems. After establishing ground rules the counsellor sits between the two clients and asks three questions to each person in turn and allows him or her each to say how they feel about the other one's answers. The questions are:

  1) What have you not liked about the other one's behaviour in the past?

  2) What have you liked about her/his behaviour in the past?

  3) How do you want this person to behave towards you in future?

  Finally the counsellor helps them agree to a workable way forward that suits them both. If the relationship is already a good one the counsellor would begin with question 2 and then question 1 before moving to question 3 (see Chapter 6 for a guide to the questions).

- *Role play* involves the group in enacting or simulating a scenario to enable skills development and practice in particular situations and the opportunity to understand the human dynamics involved. It provides a bridge between theory and practice and can be used to explore attitudes, behaviour and feelings. It is essential for role play to start within the experience of participants so that they can easily take on roles. The fictitious nature of roles and scenarios has the advantage of providing opportunities for participants to talk safely about real issues they would otherwise be reluctant to divulge.

- *Self-esteem exercises* are useful especially around bullying issues. Having good self-esteem is feeling all right about yourself and others. It is not thinking you are better or worse than others are but equal to them. Bullies and bully victims tend to have low self-esteem because bullies think they are better than others and are aggressive and victims think they are worse and behave passively. People with good self-esteem act assertively and are neither bullies nor victims. Divide students into pairs and time them two minutes each to take it in turns to tell each other: one person in the group they already feel close to and what they like about her/him, and one other person they don't know so well and what's attractive about her/him. Each person tells the group who they feel close to in this group and who they would like to get to know better and why. Ensure you and your assistant go towards the end so that anybody who has been missed out can be included.

- *Show and tells* are similar to introductions and serve the same function. Participants bring in items that they value, such as photographs, certificates, soft toys, small pieces of jewellery, artwork, poems, hobby items to show the group and talk about them in turn.

- *Support groups* are formed when the large group is divided into smaller groups of up to ten participants who usually share an identity. They split the available time in equal shares and take equal turns talking in confidence about real issues in their lives. The trainer appoints a leader in each group who ensures that each participant says a number that determines the order in which they have a turn talking. The leader calculates the number of people in the group divided by the number of minutes available to the group so each person gets equal time (usually about five minutes) being listened to. Participants in turn choose one person to be the main listener who sits next to them while the others pay attention with no interruptions. They can talk about anything or a specific issue connected with the training. Generally they talk about what's going well for them in their lives or around a specific issue, what is not going so well and how they feel about it. They finish with what they think could be their first step to improving life and/or the issue. A support group can meet regularly and build trust, or it can be part of a larger activity as a place to release some emotion about how it feels being in the larger group for example. It can help people to function better in the larger group afterwards.

Students' support group

- **Think and listens.** This provides a structure to group thinking which is an alternative to an open discussion. Each person thinks aloud about the topic in question for no more than a minute while a scribe jots down his or her ideas. No-one speaks twice until everyone has spoken once. No-one speaks three times until everyone has spoken twice and so on until the topic has been thought about sufficiently or the time runs out. The leader of the activity arranges for the ideas to be collated or summarized ready for a subsequent activity when the group will make decisions on action if necessary.

- **Throwing away the labels.** This is useful after an exercise raising awareness of stereotyping. Use a ball or a bean-bag. Get the group in a circle and ask each member to think of a label they have been given that they think is unjustified. Ask them to each throw the bean-bag one at a time into the middle of the circle. As each throws it they say the label they have chosen out loud. Then another person picks up the bean-bag from the middle, goes to their seat and then throws it saying the labelling word. The idea is to throw away the label.

- **Validations** and **self-validations** involve being honest about other people's and your own good points to build their self-esteem. Ask for a volunteer and for someone to time one minute as the trainer tells the volunteer, 'What I appreciate about you is...' while s/he replies, 'Thank you, I'm glad you've noticed.' The qualities to appreciate can be their appearance (smile, colour of hair and eyes); their attitude and approach during the training; their intelligence; their ideas; their kindness towards others; friendliness; and talents. Divide students into pairs to validate each other. Time them as they do the above in pairs and swap over after one minute. Self-validation is more effective than others telling us. Demonstrate this with another member of the group and for one minute repeat 'What I like about me is...' while the volunteer says, 'Yes, I like that about you too.' They do the above and swap over after one minute. Discuss how it felt to be giving and receiving validations. Also discuss how we have got out of the practice of doing it and why? Finish with each person sharing one thing they like about themselves.

- **Videos** can broaden the spectrum, provide perspective, impart new knowledge and illustrate skills and techniques. Although they are useful for breaking up intensive activities their prime function is meeting specific learning objectives to be reinforced after their showing.

Games

- **Fruit bowl.** Explain this is useful for mixing people up so they sit next to different people. Everyone sits on a chair in a circle and one stands in the middle. The person in the middle names each person one of four fruits such as orange, apple, kiwi fruit, banana. Then the person in the middle calls out one of the fruits and those people leave their chairs (walking rather than running when anyone in the group has mobility problems) to sit on another while the middle person tries to get on one of their chairs. The person left in the middle repeats the process. If s/he calls fruit bowl everyone gets up and changes chairs.

- **Falling game** is a trust game similar to knots (see opposite page). Demonstrate with six people in a circle with one in the middle who falls with the others supporting her/him and gently passing her/him around. Then the other groups do it with everyone having a chance to be in the middle. Afterwards discuss how it felt to be the person in the middle and the person supporting them.

- *Guess who said it*. A person goes out of the room and three people in the room tell the trainer what they like about the person outside. The trainer calls the person back in and tells her/him what was said and s/he has to guess who said each good thing. They may need clues! Repeat with one of the people who said a good thing going out next.

- *Helicopter/elephant/skunk/Viking* is an action game in a circle where the person in the middle tells one person to be a helicopter, elephant, Viking or skunk (choose actions to suit physical abilities of all the group). That person does the relevant action and the people either side contribute their actions to make a tableau of the object concerned. The person slowest completing their action or gets it wrong goes in the middle and repeats the process. Actions are: Helicopter – the middle person revolves with arms outstretched while people each side duck down; Elephant – the middle person makes a trunk with their arm while the other two form the ears with arms in circles; Skunk – the middle person bends over and waggles their bottom while the other two pinch their noses and wave their hands in disgust; and Viking – the middle person blows an imaginary horn and makes a trumpeting noise while the other two make paddling motions with imaginary oars.

- *Honey, do you love me?* The trainer says very dramatically to the person on their left 'Honey, do you love me?' trying to make them laugh. The person replies 'Honey, I love you but I just can't smile,' trying hard to keep a straight face. Then that person repeats the process with the next person. Much laughter should ensue.

- *Keys*. A person at the front or in the middle stands, eyes closed with keys behind their back. One person from the group takes the keys and speaks in a disguised voice saying, 'I am taking your keys' and then goes back to their seat. The person at the front or in the middle than has to guess who has the keys. If they do then that person goes to the front/middle and the process is repeated.

- *Knots*. This is a trust exercise similar to the falling game. Demonstrate this game with six people in a circle who with eyes shut join hands with your help. Ask them to open their eyes and then untangle themselves without letting go until they are in a circle. The rest of the group gets into groups to do this. Discuss their feelings about the exercise and which strategies worked best to untangle the knots.

Students playing knots

- *Name game one*. Introduce the soft toy and ask them to give it a name. In a circle throw a soft toy to each other calling the name of the person it is thrown to. When everyone has been called then have another round saying what they like about each person as they call their name and throw the toy.

- *Name game two*. Everyone stands up or sits down in a circle. First person says their name and makes an action. The second person says their name and makes an action and repeats first person's name and action. Repeat around the circle until everyone has repeated the names and actions of everyone.

Students playing prisoner

- *Prisoner*. 'Prisoners' sit on chairs in a circle with a 'guard' behind each one with hands ready to touch prisoners' shoulders. There are also about five empty chairs with 'guards' behind them. 'Guards' without 'prisoners' wink at 'prisoners' to release them so they can sit on their chairs. 'Prisoners' leap out of their chairs before their 'guards' can touch their shoulders. 'Guards' who lose their prisoners repeat the process. This is good for discussion afterwards about how it felt to be 'prisoner' and 'guard'.

- *Splatt* is an action game in a circle where the person in the middle points randomly at different students shouting 'Splatt!'. The person pointed at has to duck down immediately while the two on either side turn to face each other firing with their fingers as guns shouting 'Splatt!'. Out of the two, whoever gets 'Splatted' first sits down and is out of the game. The game continues until two people are left 'unsplatted'. The person in the middle sits down and the other two stand back to back for the final shoot out. The middle person calls out a number of different fruit and then a vegetable. The two finalists each take a step forward with each fruit called. When a vegetable is called they turn around quickly to 'splatt' the other and be the winner.

- *The sun shines on* is similar to fruit bowl. The person in the middle states something about themselves by saying, 'the sun shines on people with brown hair' (or, for example, has a younger brother or likes sweets). Those people with the same feature leave their chairs to sit on another while the middle person tries to get on one of their chairs. The person left in the middle repeats the process.

- *Wink murder*. There are many versions of this with the basic principle of a secret murderer(s) who winks at people to 'kill' them. Those people 'die' dramatically while detective(s) try to see who is winking. Ask the students for their favourite version and be creative in adapting it for any students with sight impairments.

- *Zoo* is the same as fruit bowl but with animals instead of fruit and students do the actions and/or sounds of the animal when they move to different chairs. Call 'zoo' for everyone to move at once.

Chapter 5

A co-counselling training course: a basis for peer listening and peer mentoring programmes

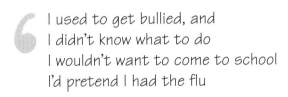

I used to get bullied, and
I didn't know what to do
I wouldn't want to come to school
I'd pretend I had the flu

But now things are so different
School's a better place to be
Because of the peer mentors
And what they did for me

Natalie Tormey
Plant Hill High School, Manchester (Moldrich and Carpentieri 2005)

There are many models of peer listening, some of which are referred to as peer counselling. The term counselling implies that peer listeners can provide a counselling service similar to one provided by qualified counsellors and it is important that this misconception is avoided in order to protect children from taking on responsibilities and tasks they are not equipped to handle. There is a need to distinguish counselling from the use of counselling skills as much for the pastoral responsibilities of teachers and school staff as for peer counsellors. After about 1998 Cowie in fact does not use the term peer counselling, to avoid confusion with formal counselling roles. She now refers to 'counselling-based approaches'. However, peer supporters can be trained in both listening and counselling skills and use these to assist others formally in an identified room at specific times, usually called a 'drop-in'. Here they offer a confidential listening service mostly on a one-to-one basis using techniques of active listening, counselling, verbal and non-verbal communication and problem solving. Staff supervise the peer listeners regularly to provide ongoing support and monitoring.

The purpose of this type of training is usually team building and improving participants' understanding of helping relationships. It is intended to promote personal development in the helpers as well as training them in the caring role. Another aim of the training is to equip the peer supporters to have a positive influence on the emotional climate of the school and to enable them to provide a bridge between troubled students in their peer group and professional counselling services.

The model of peer listening or mentoring that is chosen will depend on the aims and objectives of the project and the resources available. It is important to choose a flexible model that is adaptable to the needs of the peer listeners and users and is responsive to evaluation and monitoring. Some organizations provide helpful training guides (see Appendix 3).

The training course outlined below is based on the re-evaluation counselling model (Jackins, 1965) that has been used in 35 primary, middle, secondary and special schools. It has a co-counselling approach and covers the basic skills for preparing participants to become co-counsellors, peer listeners and/or peer mentors. Although a facilitator trained in co-counselling would be ideal, any professional with some training in counselling skills (see Chapter 4) would be able to lead this course.

Co-counselling training course

Co-counselling is when trained students take turns to counsel each other. Peer counselling in this context is when students, who have learned co-counselling, counsel untrained students one-way using the same counselling skills. Staff who learn the same model and can set up their own support groups supervise the students.

Peer counselling can take on a number of forms: older buddies or mentors for younger students; support groups; drop-ins run by peer listeners; and co-counselling clubs. To train students in co-counselling the following themes will ideally need to be addressed: listening skills; working in pairs; confidentiality; self-esteem games; leading and using a support group; supervision; and an understanding of sexism, racism, ageism and disability harassment. Relevant staff in schools also need to be trained separately or alongside the students to set up and sustain peer support systems.

The student training is the equivalent of four days and staff training is up to three days depending on the level of skills they already have. This can be shortened depending on the institution's requirements but at least two days training for students and six hours for staff is necessary. As well as running courses, Peer Support Works run workshops and support groups for students and staff from several schools to network and co-counsel with each other.

The basic student course is for 12–16 students and at least one member of staff as assistant to the main trainer. The first three days training is in one term with two follow-on sessions in each of the following two terms.

Course content and style

Courses need to be interactive and to cover the practicalities of setting up a peer support system. They need to include: teaching of counselling skills; trainer demonstrations of co-counselling; and participants practising co-counselling with each other. Strict confidentiality is essential. Students are taught, however, that should any serious disclosure (for example sexual abuse) be made the student or trainer would be bound by the Children Act to refer the disclosure to a senior member of staff. Peer supporters are taught to make this clear at the onset with any students to whom they offer support or counselling.

After the initial training in one term the students are ready to set up their peer support service immediately or in the following term with staff supervising them one session a week. If two or more schools are running a joint project they can organize joint workshops in addition to the basic training. Students and staff wishing to develop their skills further can contact Leap Peer Mediation Network and Co-Counselling International (UK) (see Appendix 3 for website addresses).

Students' course outline

- **Day 1 (6 hours)** Pre-course questionnaire; circle time; introductions; ground rules including confidentiality; games; introduction to listening and co-counselling skills; affirmations and self-validations; support groups.
- **Day 2 (6 hours)** Circle time; show and tells; more counselling skills; games; bullying; support groups.
- **Day 3 (6 hours)** Circle time; practising the peer listening session; role plays; scanning memories and other techniques and skills; games; being proud of our identities and backgrounds; plan peer support service and staff support; mid-course questionnaire.
- **Day 4 (2 hours)** Practising skills; future planning; mentoring training post-course questionnaire and evaluation.
- **Note on course games and activities**. Each of the first three days has about 20 activities of varying short lengths including games to keep up the interest and momentum for participants. They do not all have to be covered and some may take more or less time than indicated depending on the group. Trainers can select those activities most suitable for their needs. They are either outlined in Chapter 4 or explained fully in the course notes.

Day 1 (six hours)

Materials
Soft toy, pre-course questionnaires, active listening sheet, flipchart.

Aims of the session
- Group members are introduced to each other and start to form a group identity.
- Ground rules are established including confidentiality.
- Participants understand the goals of the training programme.
- Participants begin to understand the nature of co-counselling and peer listening.
- Participants learn games to help them relax, give them energy, learn for future use with other students and, last but not least, to have fun.

Activity 1   Pre-course questionnaire (see Appendix 4)

Activity 2   Opening circle — five minutes (see Chapter 4).

Activity 3   Name game one — five minutes (see Chapter 4).

Activity 4   Explain the purpose and style of the course and establish ground rules — ten minutes (see Chapter 4).

- Explain that they will learn basic co-counselling and listening skills so that (a) they can listen to and use counselling skills to help other students around bullying and other problems and (b) they can co-counsel with each other to become more self-aware and more able to listen to and counsel others. The course will be a mixture of the trainer explaining and demonstrating skills and games, the students contributing their ideas and practising their skills. Expressing and releasing feelings and emotions is good.
- Explain that the group will be working together on the course and afterwards as peer supporters so it is important for them to be co-operative, respectful, supportive and keep confidentiality. To ensure that they can work in an atmosphere of trust they will need a set of ground rules which they will all abide by.

Activity 5   Short co-counselling session — five minutes
Explain that co-counselling is a process where two people take it in turns to listen to each other for exactly the same time each way. Divide them into twos and decide who is A and who is B. Then tell them A is the listener and B the speaker. Explain that A listens to B talking about why s/he is here, what s/he wants to get out of the course and what kinds of negative and positive feelings s/he has about doing it. Time them one minute and then ask them to swap roles as listener and speaker so A has one minute to be listened to by B.

Activity 6   Short introductions — ten minutes
Everyone including trainer and staff says their names, why they are here, what they want to get out of the course and how they feel.

Activity 7   Game: Fruit bowl — five minutes (see chapter 4)

Activity 8   What is peer listening and counselling? — 20 minutes

On a flip chart ask participants to quick-think what they understand to be peer listening and counselling and what kinds of issues may be brought to the service by their peers. When they have finished, discuss each idea and introduce any areas missed out and correct any misunderstandings, especially about the difference between providing a counselling service (only professional counsellors can do this) and a peer listening service (they can do this using listening and basic counselling skills). Ensure there is a discussion about which issues would be appropriate or not for a peer listener to deal with and how they decide when a referral should be made and how to do it. Invite questions so far.

Break — 15 minutes

Activity 9   Explain what co-counselling is — five minutes (see Chapter 4)

Activity 10   Counselling skills: Giving attention — 15 minutes

- Explain the importance of the counsellor creating a safe environment for the client to feel able to discuss problems. They will need to prepare a quiet room or space where there is some privacy and no interruptions. Two chairs of the same size need to face each other about 60 cm apart. The counsellor sits on one chair and the client the other. The counsellor leans slightly forward with hands resting open on her lap though s/he can offer to hold the client's hand if the client looks in need of comfort. S/he keeps relaxed eye contact and does not move around or fidget.

- Split participants into pairs with A as client and B as counsellor. A tells B about something she enjoyed doing recently for two minutes and B does not listen though stays seated.

- Ask all the As how it felt not to be listened to and to say what B did that showed s/he wasn't. Write the responses on a flip chart or whiteboard.

- Swap roles so A listens attentively to B for two minutes. Ask all the Bs how they felt and what the As were doing to show they were listening. Write on the flip chart or whiteboard.

- Talk about non-verbal communication and how important it is to be aware of our body language.

Do

Make eye contact

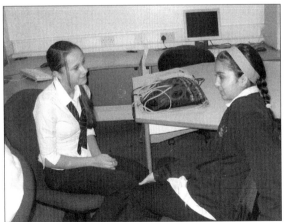
Pay attention to the client

Don't

Not look at the client

Ignore them

Activity 11   Counselling skills: Active listening — ten minutes (see Chapter 4)

The point of co-counselling is to enable each other to discharge feelings and emotions in a counselling session rather than in everyday life where uncontrolled expression of emotions at inappropriate times can cause confusion, disruption and perpetuate problems. Explain the importance of: concentrating on what is being said and how, as well as noticing the feelings that are behind what is said. Point out that the following obstacles must be avoided:

a)   Thinking of how to respond.

b)   Trying to think of a solution.

c)   Asking too many questions.

d)   Making assumptions on what is said.

e)   Being reminded of and thinking about a similar situation in your own life.

Activity 12   Game: Wink murder — five minutes (see Chapter 4)

Activity 13   Demonstration do's and don'ts of co-counselling with your assistant — ten minutes

- How not to do it. The trainer shows them how not to counsel the assistant who is trying to tell her/him how s/he is a good listener and what s/he finds difficult. This will involve looking around the room in a bored fashion, fidgeting, interrupting, talking about her or himself, asking the client to discuss something s/he doesn't want to talk about, giving advice in a brusque manner, being cloyingly sympathetic and other inappropriate behaviour. (The assistant will need good humour for this and expect much laughter from the group.)

- How to do it. The trainer swaps over and the assistant will show them how to do it properly by listening attentively to her/him talk on the same subject. This will involve relaxed eye contact, facing the trainer with open body language, delighted and interested facial expression, encouragement and asking about feelings.

- The trainer asks the group what s/he did wrong and what the assistant did right. Discuss the difference it makes to a person's feelings when listened to properly.

Activity 14   In pairs co-counsel each other — ten minutes

- The trainer divides the group into pairs A and B and explains they will take turns as client and counsellor and will time them three minutes each way. When they are the client they can talk about what listening they do, to whom and where; what's difficult about listening; and in what way they are a good listener. When counselling they use the do's on the active listening sheet (Chapter 4). The trainer and assistant can co-counsel together or walk around ready to help if they get stuck.

- When each person has had their three minutes they get back into a circle and ask each person to say in what situations or to what kinds of people do they find listening difficult and what they are good at. They can use the sheets as a guide.

Activity 15   Self-esteem exercises — 25 minutes (see Chapter 4)

Activity 16   Validations and self-validations — 15 minutes (see Chapter 4)

Lunch — one hour

Activity 17   More counselling skills — Asking questions — 30 minutes

- The counsellor's task is to enable the client to explore their situation, identify the main problem, gain a clearer understanding of it and decide what to do. In order to promote this the counsellor needs to ask open questions which do not invite yes, no or one word answers (which are responses to closed questions). Open questions begin with: who; what; when; where; and how. Avoid asking 'why' as that could imply that the counsellor thinks the client is to blame in some way for what happened or how they feel.

- The trainer explains that beginners sometimes interrupt the client too often with questions, or ask too many, sometimes two at a time, and this can give the client a feeling of confusion or even interrogation. This is usually the result of feeling uncomfortable with a silence. It is fine for a client to be silent and if the counsellor interrupts it is better to offer validations rather than a rapid succession of questions.

- The group is divided into threes with A as counsellor, B as client and C as observer. A spends two minutes using both open and closed questions to ask B about her/his hobbies and listens to the responses. B then feeds back which questions helped her explore the subject and which closed down the conversation. C notes down the examples of open and closed questions. Repeat so that each participant has a turn being counsellor, client and observer. Finally the groups reconvene so they can report back their examples of open and closed questions which are written on the flipchart.

Activity 18   Game: Knots — ten minutes (see Chapter 4)

Explain how open questions can help people untangle the knots in their problems.

Activity 19   Support groups — 35 minutes (see Chapter 4)

Discuss what's going well for them and /or a situation not going well and how they feel about it. The students each finish with what they think could be their first step to improving life and/or the issue even more.

Activity 20   Appreciations and arranging co-counselling practice — five minutes

- In the whole group each person says who counselled them and what they did well.
- Each student chooses a co-counselling partner and arranges at least one co-counselling session before the next training day (anything between five and 15 minutes each way). They can talk about whatever issue is important to them in their session or talk about what has gone well during the week, what hasn't gone so well and what is their next step forward.

Activity 21   Closing circle — five minutes

Ask them to bring in Show and tells (see Chapter 4) next time. Then each person says a highlight from the day and something they like about the person on their left.

Day 2 (six hours)

Materials
Active listening sheet, ground rules from day 1.

Aims of the session:
- Introduce more listening and counselling skills.
- Participants share 'show and tells'.
- Discussions about bullying.
- Practise counselling skills in support groups.
- Participants learn more games.

Activity 1   Opening circle — five minutes

Activity 2   Name game two — ten minutes (see Chapter 4)

Activity 3   Refresher from first day — ten minutes
Recap confidentiality, and listening and counselling skills using a flip chart and asking participants to identify the different aspects covered on day 1.

Activity 4   Co-counselling sessions — 15 minutes
- In pairs take turns of four minutes each to talk about what went well/not so well this week and their next step.
- Ask each person to say what his or her co-counsellors did well in this last session or in the session since day 1. Any questions about the co-counselling process?

Activity 5   Show and tells — ten minutes
Five volunteers each take a few minutes to talk about and display their 'show and tells'.

Activity 6   Reflecting — 15 minutes
Explain that a counsellor can notice what the feelings are behind the client's words and body language and reflect them back so that the client can talk more about their feelings and perhaps release them. For example:

Client: In school today my best friend went off with this other girl at break and ignored me.
Counsellor: It sounds like you are feeling angry about her.

Using the flip chart write a few already prepared client statements similar to the above and ask students in pairs to identify the feelings behind each one and a suitable response. Then the group reconvenes to share ideas.

Activity 7   Game: The sun shines on — five minutes (see chapter 4)

Activity 8   Paraphrasing — 20 minutes

This is similar to reflecting. The counsellor pinpoints the most important issue in the client's statements, and rephrases it back to the client more briefly and in her or his own words. This shows that the counsellor is listening and the client will feel encouraged to expand further, discharge feelings and understand the problem more clearly. For example:

Client: My sister comes into my room without asking and breaks my things and when I shout at her to stop she cries and tells my parents that I hit her and gets me into trouble. They always believe her and I'm the one who gets told off.
Counsellor: It sounds like you feel your parents aren't being fair.

Divide the group into threes with A as client, B as counsellor and C as observer. A tells B about her/his weekend activities while B listens and uses open questions, reflecting and paraphrasing to help A along. C observes and notes down every instance of open question, reflecting and paraphrasing. After four minutes C feeds back to A and B and then they rotate so each person has each role in turn. The whole group reconvenes to discuss the processes focusing on what was easy and what was difficult.

Break — 15 minutes

Activity 9   Five Show and tells — ten minutes

Activity 10   Empathy — ten minutes

Explain that an empathic counsellor puts herself in the place of the client in order to understand her/his point of view. S/he then conveys this understanding to the client by responding in a way that shows an awareness of the client's feelings as well as his/her words.

For example:
Client: I'm really worried about my headaches and I can't sleep at nights. I'm taking too much on. I'm in the school play, the cricket team and Young Enterprise. I know I should give something up but I can't decide which one as each teacher wants me to do their thing and I can't let them down.

Beginners sometimes find it hard to show empathy and confuse it with other, unhelpful responses. Ask them which of the following responses show: identification; sympathy; lack of sympathy; and empathy:

- I know what you mean – I was like that in Year 8. (Identification)
- I feel really sorry for you – those teachers are being unfair putting on so much pressure. (Sympathy)
- It's about time you sorted this out. Chill out! (Lack of sympathy)
- It sounds like life is stressful and hard at the moment and the headaches and sleepless nights must be making it difficult for you to think about what to do. (Empathy)

Activity 11   Dealing with feelings — five minutes

Explain how our own feelings about various issues can get in the way of our listening to clients when they talk about those particular issues. Instead of empathizing we are drawn towards identifying, sympathizing or even worse not sympathizing. It is important that we provide ourselves with opportunities in co-counselling sessions to discharge our own feelings about various issues so that we are in a better position to think more clearly and effectively empathize with clients.

Activity 12   Game: Splatt — five minutes (see Chapter 4)

Activity 13   Bullying problems — 20 minutes

(For those training to be peer mentors suggest they use this exercise as a model for a peer education lesson on bullying with their future mentees in Year 7.) Bullying is an issue that arouses many feelings. Explain how important it is to show empathy when listening to clients who are bullied or who bully. Raise awareness by asking participants to quick think using four headings on a flip chart: What is bullying? Who gets targeted? Why do people bully? How does it make us feel? Discuss in what way is the bullying more to do with the bully than the victim. Ask them to suggest useful and effective anti-bullying strategies.

Lunch — one hour

Activity 14   Opening circle — five minutes

Everyone says something they enjoyed over lunchtime.

Activity 15   Support groups — 40 minutes

- The trainer demonstrates counselling someone in the group who has a memory of bullying either as a victim or observer. Ask them to tell the story of what happened, how they felt and what they did well in the situation. Use empathy to show understanding of the client's point of view and validations and self-validations to raise self-esteem. If the client cries, laughs or gets angry allow this to happen and encourage it. Get their attention back to the present at the end by asking a silly question such as 'invent a new flavour for crisps' or 'spell your name backwards'.

- Divide into two groups as in day 1 and adult leaders swap over groups. Ensure each person, including the adult, takes a turn to talk on earliest memories of bullying. Each person chooses one person to sit next to him or her and counsel them when it is their turn while the rest listen. Counsellors counsel each client for five minutes, using all the techniques especially open questions, empathy, validations and encourage the client to self-validate. The whole group reconvenes and each person says what their counsellor did well, specifying particular techniques.

Activity 16   Game: Zoo — five minutes (see chapter 4)

Activity 17   Four Show and tells — ten minutes

Activity 18   Positive regard — 20 minutes

Counsellors need to show this to their clients. Talk about how human beings naturally have positive regard and love towards each other. Discuss with them the limitless ways we have of creating a loving relationship. The ability to give and feel love is often more essential to our survival than being loved. When people show us anything other than love they are really showing us something that's hurting – a distress within them – that is getting in the way. With counselling clients who feel unloved it is important to show your positive regard of them and that you like them. Also help them to scan memories of when they have been loved.

Demonstrate memory scanning with a volunteer starting with their earliest memory of loving and being loved and gradually working forwards through their life with memories of family, friends, animals and so on who loved them or who they loved. Encourage the release of feelings by asking open questions, empathizing and other techniques as you help them scan their memories.

In pairs practise counselling skills by helping each other scan memories as above for five minutes each way.

Activity 19   Game: Honey, do you love me? — ten minutes (see Chapter 4)

Activity 20   Closing circle

Ensure the students all book a co-counselling session with partners. Then each person say a highlight from the day and appreciate the person on the right by saying what they like about her/him.

Day 3 (six hours)

Materials
Notepads and pen/pencil, mid-course questionnaires, 14 sheets of A4, felt tip pens, pins and pincushion.

Aims of the session:
- Introduce more listening and counselling skills.
- Practise a peer listening session.
- Discussions about identity, culture and backgrounds.
- Practise counselling skills in support groups.
- Plan peer support service and staff support.
- Learn more games.
- Evaluate effect of the course so far.

Activity 1   Opening circle — five minutes
They each name their favourite game either now or in the past.

Activity 2   Game: Falling game — five minutes (see Chapter 4)

Activity 3   Outline plan for the day and refresher from days 1 and 2 — ten minutes
Recap confidentiality and listening and counselling skills using flipchart notes from day 2 refresher activity and ask participants to identify the different aspects covered on day 2.

Activity 4   Summarizing — five minutes
Explain this is similar to paraphrasing but consists of several statements rather than one. The counsellor sums up the client's feelings and the main points s/he has made. This shows

the counsellor has really grasped what she's been told and gives the client a chance to correct her if s/he has not.

Activity 5   Identity, culture and backgrounds — 30 minutes

Talk about how our identities are made up of many features such as: our gender; age; talents; places we come from; culture; social class; abilities; and jobs we do. We are unique, yet also have features in common with others. Explain how people are often targeted and made to feel ashamed of aspects of their identity, especially unchangeable ones, such as disabilities, racial origin and gender but also aspects they can change like music tastes and hobbies. Therefore it is important to be proud of our identities, backgrounds and preferences. Ask them to quick-think identities that get targeted and write on the flip chart. Ensure race, nationality, where they live, culture, social class, religion, ability and sexuality are included as well as physical abilities, characteristics, clothes, music tastes and interests. Explain how the targeting originates from outside the group and then becomes internalized within it and within each person in the group, using the diagrams below.

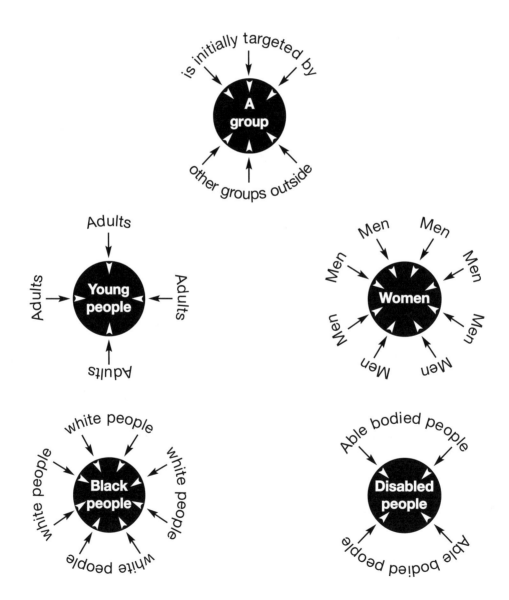

Split the group into pairs with someone they do not usually counsel with to take turns, two minutes each, talking about all the identities they have such as female, white, Welsh, clever at maths, from single parent family and dancer. They finish by saying which ones they are most proud of. After each session the counsellor summarizes to the client the main points of what s/he has said and felt.

The trainer asks for a volunteer and counsels them in front of the group on the aspects of their identity, culture, family background and other features focusing on what they are proud of. Choose one they feel especially proud of and what they never again want to hear said against that group. Summarize what has been said and felt back to the client for them to have a chance to agree or disagree.

Activity 6   Support groups — 35 minutes
As in day 1 and 2, each person has three minutes to talk to their chosen counsellor while the rest listen. Counsellor uses skills learned in day 1 and 2 repeats the identity counselling demonstrated by the trainer at the end of Activity 5 (They have approximately five minutes each.)

Break — 15 minutes

Activity 7   Game — Prisoner — five minutes (see Chapter 4)

Activity 8   Three stages in peer counselling — five minutes
Summarize the three stages of the peer counselling process as follows:

1. *Identify problem*. Build a relationship with the client by giving full attention, listening well, showing positive regard and respect. Look confident and happy with the client. Help the client explore and identify any problems and their emotions about them.

2. *Encourage release of feelings and understanding*. Use counselling techniques of active listening, validations, paraphrasing and summary. This is to help and encourage the client to explore and release emotions connected to the problem/s so s/he can re-evaluate feelings and understand the problem more objectively.

3. *Enable action planning*. Help client to identify goals and think about possible courses of action and their consequences. Encourage the client to follow up the session with at least one clear activity towards reaching her/his goals. Offer another session where this action can be evaluated and further counselling can be offered if necessary.

Explain this is a general guide to help with structuring the session but the counsellor needs to think quickly and flexibly as sometimes it doesn't follow that order. For example stage 1 may be skipped with the client entering stage 2 immediately by bursting into tears. This discharge will need to be encouraged fully before the client can move to stage 3 to think and talk clearly about the problem and plan subsequent action. Having done that the client may need to move back to stage 2, talk about the feelings and release more emotions connected to the actions s/he is planning.

Activity 9   The peer counselling session — five minutes
Explain that the peer counsellors will have up to 30 minutes in each session depending on the time constraints in school. The session will have a clear beginning, middle and end, though not necessarily of equal length. Peer listeners need to:

- Prepare the room and chairs beforehand to ensure privacy and no interruptions.
- Introduce themselves to the client and say how long the session can last.
- Explain confidentiality and the possibility of referral.

- Identify and explore the problem.
- Encourage release of feelings and understanding of the problem.
- Help with action planning.
- Ask whether the client wants another session and arrange it if necessary.
- End the session.

Activity 10 Summarizing the components of a peer listening session — ten minutes

Quick-think the following on a flip chart:

- active listening skills
- positive regard
- validations
- empathy
- emotional discharge
- open questions
- summarizing
- paraphrasing
- confidentiality
- setting up and structure of the session.

Activity 11 Preparation for role plays — ten minutes

In pairs take turns as peer counsellors and clients in different role-play situations while everyone watches supportively. This is important for practice and assessment of each person's suitability as a peer counsellor. In the box below are some examples of role plays but it is best for students and staff to use real situations and issues especially relevant to their school. Include as wide a variety of issues as possible. Either prepare these earlier or the students work out their role play just before their turn or as they are doing it. Remind them about confidentiality. Give out two role plays to each pair randomly and ask if they want to swap them around or make up their own. One pair can swap role plays with another pair, if they wish, so they feel comfortable with the role plays they will be enacting.

Examples of role-play situations

▶ You are in Year 7 and since starting the school in September you have spent most of your time with your two best friends from primary school. However, they have started spending time with another group and don't want to be friends with you any more. You feel very upset and lonely and feel that everyone else has their groups of friends and you are left out. It makes you not want to come to school and would prefer to stay at home if your mum would let you.

▶ You are in Year 10. There are some students selling cannabis around the corner from the school and all your friends are buying some and are pressurizing you to join in. You are afraid they'll exclude you from the group if you don't.

▶ You are in Year 11 aged 15 and are really scared because you had unprotected sex yesterday and are terrified of being pregnant. You've heard of the morning-after pill but don't know where to get it. You're scared of going to the doctor or school nurse in case they tell your parents.

> ‣ You are in Year 8 and small for your age. It feels like everyone in Year 8 is laughing at you because of your short stature. They call you 'titch' and other names which you don't like. You try to ignore it but you are getting very upset and don't know what to do about it.
>
> ‣ You are 16 in the spring term of year 11 and the exams are coming up. You didn't do very well in the mock exams before Christmas and your parents are nagging you as well as the teachers. You are behind with your coursework and feel panicky and hopeless about the whole thing. You feel like leaving school at Easter and not doing the exams at all but your parents won't let you.

Activity 12   Acting out role-play sessions — 30 minutes

- Divide the group into two groups with three pairs in each and an adult leading each group. In each group the adult ensures the following takes place.

- Begin with the first two volunteers, one being the counsellor and the other the client. While the counsellor sets up the chairs and the rest of the group arrange themselves in a semi-circle in front of them, the client prepares to enact their chosen role play. There will only be time for ten minutes each session so it will not be exactly the same as a real session that could be longer. Also if the counsellor gets stuck the trainer can intervene and invite the rest of the group to make suggestions on how to move the session on. Have a large sheet in view with the following written on it to help the listener:

  1. Introduce yourself to the client and say how long the session can last.
  2. Explain confidentiality and the possibility of referral.
  3. Identify and explore the problem.
  4. Encourage release of feelings and understanding of the problem.
  5. Help with action planning.
  6. Ask whether client wants another session and arrange it if necessary.
  7. End the session.

- After the session ask the client to de-role (say how it felt to be pretending the role or to be talking about a real problem) and for feedback on how helpful the process was and what could have been better. Then ask the peer listener what went well and what s/he could have done differently.

- Swap over so the client now is the listener and the listener the client and repeat the process with a different role play.

Activity 13   Set up role plays for the other two pairs in the afternoon session — 15 minutes

Lunch — one hour

Activity 14   Opening circle — five minutes
Participants say one thing they like about being the age they are

Activity 15   Finish role plays — 45 minutes
Proceed as before lunch with the remaining two pairs of students and a game after the first pair.

Activity 16   Game: Guess who said it — five minutes (see Chapter 4)

Activity 17   Plan peer support programme — 30 minutes

- Explain the role of the staff supervisors and the administrative systems and recording forms that will be needed to run a peer counselling and listening service.

- Think and listens with a scribe. Each person thinks aloud about the questions below while a scribe jots down their ideas. No-one speaks twice until everyone has spoken once.

- Questions:
  1. What form will the service take (Mentors to Year 7? Co-counselling club? Drop-in service).
  2. Name for their service?(see box below for ideas)
  3. What role would each person like to play in the service?
  4. When can supervision meetings with teacher/s take place?
  5. Publicity?

- Decisions on dates and next steps towards setting up the service.

- Give out monitoring sheets and explain how to fill in (see Chapter 9).

What can you call your project?

Here are examples of names adopted by various peer support projects:

- ABC (Anti-Bullying Committee)
- ACHE (Advice, Care, Help, Empathy) Befriending Scheme
- Buddies
- EAR4U
- FAB (Fighting Against Bullying)
- The Goodfellas
- Guardian Angels
- Helpline 2004
- Listening Service
- PALS (Pupils Always Listening Scheme)
- PLP (Peer Listening Project)
- SOS (Students' Own Support)
- SSS (Student Support Service)

Activity 18   Appreciations on backs — 20 minutes (see Chapter 4)

Activity 19   Evaluations — five minutes (see Chapter 9)

Activity 20   Closing circle — five minutes

Ensure they have co-counselling partners and book their next session then each person says one highlight from the three days and what the trainer/s did well.

Finish — Give out certificates (see opposite) now or at a later date.

School

Peer Support Project

This is to certify that

Attended an 18 hour counselling skills course
over three days at

and satisfied the course requirements

Counselling Teacher

Date of Issue

Day 4 (two hours)

Aims of the session

Group members: practise co-counselling skills; learn mentoring training; relationship counselling; and plan for the future.

Activity 1   Opening circle — five minutes

Activity 2   Plan for the session — five minutes

- Practise counselling.
- Discuss progress as mentors so far and troubleshoot if necessary.
- Learn relationship counselling as a form of mediation.
- Think about your next steps in the peer support service.

Activity 3   Counselling sessions — ten minutes

Each person talks about what's been enjoyable/easy as peer supporters/mentors and what's been difficult.

Activity 4   Game — five minutes

The keys game (see Chapter 4).

Activity 5   Discuss progress so far — 15 minutes

Ask participants to explain what they've been doing so far as mentors/peer supporters, the drop-in and co-counselling with each other. Each group talks about their activities. Iron out any problems.

Activity 6   Relationship counselling — five minutes

Briefly explain the process and its purpose.

Activity 7   Demonstrate with two people — ten minutes

Ask for two volunteers who want to get closer, improve their relationship and/or resolve past or current problems between them. Demonstrate the process with them.

Activity 8   Practise relationship counselling — 15 minutes

Divide the group into threes, name each person A, B, C and ask them to do the exercise opposite.

- A counsels B and C for five minutes
- B counsels A and C for five minutes
- C counsels A and B for five minutes.

Relationship counselling

Explain you are neutral and will not take sides. Ask each person to agree not to interrupt each other. Ask the following questions to each person in turn:

1. ▶ Ask A what have you not liked about B's behaviour in the past.
   ▶ Ask B how s/he feels about what A has just said.

   ▶ Ask B what have you not liked about A's behaviour in the past.
   ▶ Ask A how s/he feels about what B has just said.

2. ▶ Ask A what have you liked about B's behaviour in the past.
   ▶ Ask B how s/he feels about what A has just said.

   ▶ Ask B what have you liked about A's behaviour in the past.
   ▶ Ask A how s/he feels about what B has just said.

3. ▶ Ask A how s/he wants B's behaviour to be in the future.
   ▶ Ask B how s/he feels about what A has just said.

   ▶ Ask B how s/he wants A's behaviour to be in the future.
   ▶ Ask A how s/he feels about what B has just said.

4. Get an agreement on future behaviours and ask them to shake hands.

Break — 15 minutes

Activity 9   Discuss the process of relationship counselling — five minutes
Also plan how it can be used as a mediation service for students in school.

Activity 10   Game — five minutes

Activity 11   Demonstrate counselling — five minutes
Ask for a volunteer and counsel them on what they loved/hated about being 11 years old/ being in Year 7 and what they would have liked from a mentor if they had one.

Activity 12   In pairs take turns — ten minutes
Participants take turns counselling each other on what they loved/hated about being 11 years old/ being in Year 7 and what they would have liked from a mentor if they had one.

Activity 13   Share — five minutes
Each person talks about the above in a round.

Activity 14   Closing circle — five minutes
Each person appreciates their co-counselling partner and books a co-counselling session with a partner.

Chapter 6

A conflict resolution training course: a basis for peer mediation programmes

 Everybody has won and all must have prizes.

(Lewis Carroll)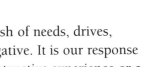

Conflict is a natural and inevitable part of life that arises from a clash of needs, drives, wishes and/or demands. In itself conflict is neither positive nor negative. It is our response to conflict that transforms it into either a competitive and often destructive experience or a constructive challenge offering opportunities for co-operation and growth. When conflict is understood it can become an opportunity to learn and create.

Conflict resolution programmes have been used worldwide at all levels ranging from peacemaking in war torn countries to sorting out disputes in school playgrounds. It is inevitable that students get into fights, arguments or disagreements and that it affects school life in some way. However, these disputes do not have to be unproductive or lead to unproductive consequences, like time away from class and increased stress and tension. In schools conflict resolution programmes can promote both the individual behavioural change needed for responsible citizenship and the systemic change necessary for a safe learning environment. The purpose of conflict resolution programmes in schools is twofold: to teach students from diverse backgrounds basic healthy communication skills, and to develop whole-school systems in which communication skills can be applied and modelled. Conflict resolution programmes aim to instil the values of tolerance and peacemaking among students as they become empowered to resolve conflicts that arise in schools.

Peer mediation

Peer mediation is a specific form of conflict resolution that empowers students to mediate peer disputes that can often get in the way of classroom learning and school safety. At a time when adults look to young people to solve their own problems without constant adult supervision, peer mediation is an effective way for schools to decrease violence and increase student empowerment and community service. Peer mediators are trained to be neutral third parties assisting their peers in resolving conflicts peacefully. They do not counsel or give advice and are trained to hear all sides of a dispute, ask questions and facilitate a resolution. The process is formal and disputants are asked to sign a set of ground rules before the mediation can proceed. At the conclusion of the process, disputants write and sign an agreement.

Children from Year 4 upwards can be trained in mediation skills and both primary and secondary schools can use peer mediators. To develop peer mediation successfully requires a whole-school approach and an investment of time and money in the initial training. The benefits to schools often include the lessening of violent or aggressive methods of handling conflict and an increase in the personal responsibility of students.

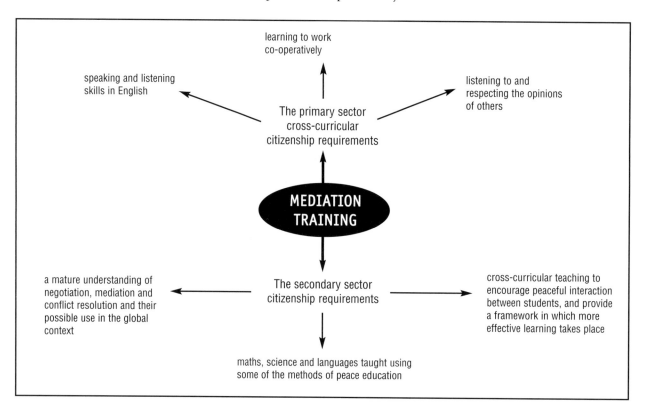

To ensure the programme meets the needs of all students, mediators are chosen from as many diverse backgrounds and abilities as possible. They learn to work as a team to resolve personal and interpersonal conflicts by intervening and resolving conflict productively. Mediators assume responsibility for their own conflicts and do not encourage or intervene in school fights. Instead they recognize conflict and intervene in the early stages by referring disputants to mediation. The ability to resolve disputes peacefully is central to the expression of human rights and is essential to school life. Building effective relationships among school students is important both for reaching agreements and for shaping how they choose to disagree

The role of peer mediation

Many conflicts in schools arise from differences. Cultural conflicts are based on national origin or ethnicity. Social conflicts are based on gender, sexual orientation, social class and physical and academic abilities. Reactions to differences often manifest as prejudice, discrimination, harassment and sometimes hate crimes. These complex conflicts are rooted in prejudice, discrimination, inequality and privilege. Conflict resolution and mediation programmes provide a framework for addressing these problems by promoting respect and acceptance through new ways of communicating with and understanding others. However, peer mediators cannot mediate every kind of conflict and by identifying the type of conflict they can concentrate on, those disputes can be better managed (see Appendix 5: Handout 1 and the box below).

Conflict situations where peer mediators can help

Low level disputes like: alleged theft from a student; name calling; low level bullying; 'play' arguments; teasing; attention seeking behaviour; friends falling out; relationship arguments; rumour-spreading; and ostracizing.

Three girls ostracizing another

Teasing about trainers

Conflict situations where peer mediators will need to refer to adults

Violent conflict such as hitting, punching, tripping, spitting, hair pulling, use of weapons, gang fights and other forms of physical fighting and/or bullying. After these have been dealt with, usually with sanctions, peer mediation can be used to rebuild relationships between disputants.

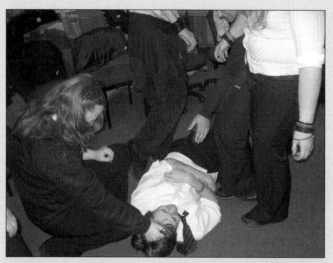

Bully gang

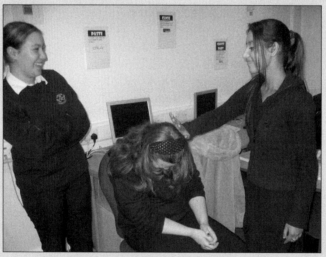

Hitting

Racial, sexual, homophobic and disability harassment cannot be tolerated and although peer mediators can help in non-violent situations they are best used to rebuild relationships after sanctions have taken place.

Schools alone cannot change violence in society but young people can be equipped by them to act responsibly and to understand and accept the consequences of their behaviour. Through mediation and conflict resolution young people can gain the knowledge, abilities and processes to choose alternatives to self-destructive and violent behaviour when confronted with conflict in their lives.

The context for peer mediation

A precondition to successful mediation is a no-blame approach to antisocial behaviour and conflicts. Mediation taking place within this type of whole-school climate has more chance of success. The most helpful working assumption is that nobody is born wishing to harm others. For example bullying behaviour has been learned by children from a very young age from the older people around them, so the most useful work with bullies will focus on its being unlearned. They need to learn that aggressive behaviour is not acceptable. Many witness deliberate acts of physical and verbal aggression in their homes, in school, their environment and on television and films. It is not surprising that by the time they go to infant school they have learned many ways of bullying others often by being bullied themselves. They need to be taught the appropriate social behaviour that may not be in their repertoire of social skills. They need to be enabled to understand the feelings, strengths and behaviour of other people.

The following training session for volunteer peer mediators is designed to take place within a school promoting a 'no blame' ethos and should be delivered by qualified school staff and adapted to the school's needs.

Conflict resolution course

Preparation

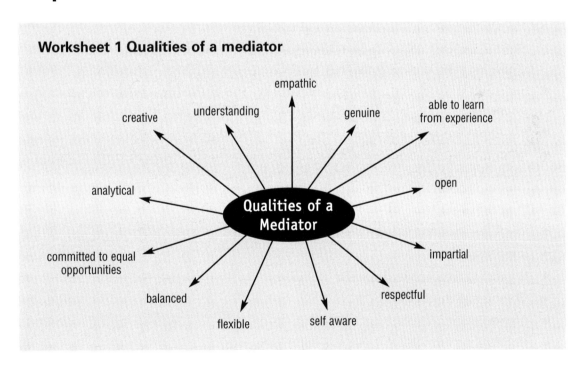

Worksheet 1 Qualities of a mediator

Chapter 5 outlines the steps required for setting up any peer support project. A particularly important step for a mediation project is the recruiting of trainees as it will determine its nature, scope, and success. A combination of application forms, interviews and positive selection with peer and/or adult nominations to ensure a balance of gender, race, and physical and academic ability would probably be the most successful method of recruitment. It is important that students have, or have the potential to acquire, as many of the above qualities as possible. It is also important to create supporting roles for students who apply but are not selected for training (see Chapter 4).

Course content and style

Courses need to be interactive and to cover the practicalities of setting up a peer mediation service. They need to include: teaching of mediation skills; trainer demonstrations of mediation; and participants practising mediation with each other. Strict confidentiality is essential.

After the initial three days training set out below, the students are ready to set up their mediation service immediately or in the subsequent term with staff supervision one session a week. After one term the students will need the further three hour session to troubleshoot, refresh, reflect, add skills and make future plans. If two or more schools are running a joint project they can organize joint workshops in addition to the basic training. Students and staff wishing to develop their skills further can contact the Leap Peer Mediation Network (see Appendix 3 for website addresses).

Students' course outline

An overview

Every session will begin and end with circle time and include mediation practice, role plays, demonstrations and games. The focus in each session will be as follows:

Day 1 (six hours)

- Pre-course questionnaire
- Introductions and ground rules including confidentiality
- Introduction to conflict resolution and mediation
- What a mediator does – active listening; handling emotions; validations; role play a mediation session on negotiation
- Skills and qualities of a mediator – impartiality and hearing two sides; empathy not sympathy
- Circumstances most and least favourable for mediation
- What mediation can and cannot do: conflict management styles; destructive and constructive conflict

Day 2 (six hours)

- Conflict – breaking unhelpful cycles
- Support groups
- Separating facts and feelings
- Communication blockers
- Questionnaire
- Building rapport – helpful and unhelpful behaviour

Day 3 (six hours)

- Non-verbal communication between cultures
- Stereotypes and prejudice – anti-bullying, sexism, racism and able-bodyism awareness raising
- Taking pride in identities

- Mediation practice – setting the scene, hearing the issues, exploring the issues; building agreements, closure and follow-up
- Plan mediation service and staff support
- Mid-course questionnaire

Day 4 (three hours)
- Discuss progress so far
- Dealing with difficult situations during mediation sessions
- Relationship counselling
- Future planning
- Monitoring
- End of training evaluation
- Signing of contacts
- Certificates

Note on course games and activities. Each of the first three days has about 20 activities of varying short lengths including games to keep up the interest and momentum for participants. They do not all have to be covered and some may take more or less time than indicated depending on the group. Select those most suitable from the activities outlined in Chapter 5 and those explained fully in the course notes in this chapter.

Detailed plan

Day 1 (six hours)

Materials
Soft toy, pre-course questionnaires, active listening skills sheet (chapter 4), flip chart.

Aims of the session
Group members:
- are introduced to each other and start to form a group identity.
- agree to ground rules including confidentiality.
- understand the goals of the training programme.
- begin to understand the nature of conflict resolution and mediation.
- learn games to help them relax, give them energy and to have fun.

Activity 1   Pre-course questionnaire – ten minutes (see Appendix 4)

Activity 2   Opening circle – five minutes (see Chapter 4)

Activity 3   Name game one – five minutes (see Chapter 4)

Activity 4   Explain the purpose and style of the course and establish ground rules — ten minutes

- Explain briefly what conflict resolution is at international and playground level and that mediation is a process in which an outsider is invited by people with a dispute to help them come to a solution that they can agree on. The disputants, not the mediator, decide the terms of this agreement. Mediators do not take sides or offer their own solutions, but listen to both sides of the story, including the feelings involved, and allow the disputants to find ways forward. Peer mediation is the method of enabling young people to mediate the conflicts among those of their own age and background.

- Explain that they will learn basic mediation skills so that (a) they can listen to and use mediation skills to help other students resolve any conflicts or disputes in school and (b) they can mediate each other if they have any disputes among themselves and become more self-aware. The course will be a mixture of the trainer explaining and demonstrating skills and games, and them contributing their ideas and practising their skills. Expressing and releasing feelings and emotions is good.

- Explain that the group will be working together on the course and afterwards as peer mediators so it is important for them to be co-operative, respectful, supportive and keep confidentiality. To ensure that they can work in an atmosphere of trust they will need a set of ground rules which they will all abide by (see Chapter 4).

Activity 5   Coloured ribbons — ten minutes (see Chapter 4)

Give ribbons out to each person to get a partner. In pairs take it in turns to listen to each other talk about what they do to relax, why they chose to do peer mediation and how they feel about it. Time them one minute and then ask them to swap roles as listener and speaker.

Activity 6   Short introductions — ten minutes

Everyone including trainer and staff says their names, what they do to relax and why they chose to do the peer mediation course and how they feel.

Activity 7   Game: Fruit bowl — five minutes (see Chapter 4)

Activity 8   Active listening — 15 minutes (see Chapter 4)

Working in pairs they choose one of the following topics to talk about for three minutes: my favourite day out, hobby, music, TV programmes, dreams, a childhood memory. One speaks while the other listens. The listener can use questions to draw out the speaker. After three minutes the listener feeds back accurately the facts and feelings. Then the roles reverse.

Activity 9   Validations — 15 minutes (see Chapter 4)

Break — 15 minutes

Activity 10   Empathy: exploring different perceptions of the same event — ten minutes

Read out loud *The Maligned Wolf* (see Appendix 5, Handout 2). Ask them what this story is (Red Riding Hood story from the wolf's point of view). Ensure there is a discussion to cover the following:
- How did that differ from the story with which we are familiar?
- Do we often look at something from only one point of view, and if we do does it matter?

- Is there always more than one side of a story?
- Explain peer mediation is hearing both or all points of view and being neutral. Invite questions so far.

Activity 11   The story of Red Riding Hood and the Wolf retold through mediation — 20 minutes

Divide the class into groups of four who discuss how two mediators could resolve the problems between Red Riding Hood and the Wolf. Then they assign roles to 'Red', 'Wolf' and two mediators who practise their mediation for ten minutes. The trainer needs to ensure the role players sit in a square with to 'Red' and 'Wolf' each having a mediator sitting next them.

Activity 12   Identifying the skills of a mediator — 15 minutes

Give to each group of four copies the Mediation skills chart (shown on Worksheet 2). Ask the group to identify where Red's and Wolf's mediators were using the skills shown on the chart.

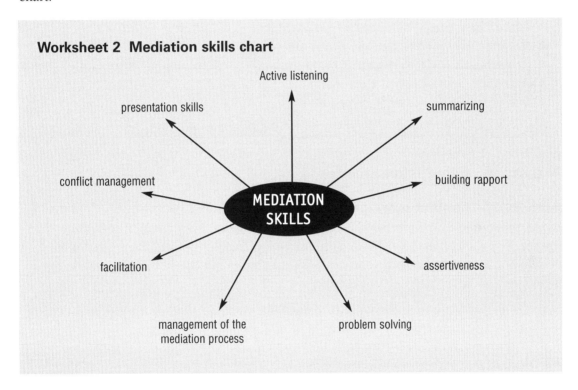

Worksheet 2 Mediation skills chart

Ask each group to report back their findings to the whole class.

Activity 13   Identifying the qualities of a mediator — ten minutes

Divide the group into pairs and give out a mediators, qualities chart (see Worksheet 1 earlier in this chapter) to each person. Each person will tell the other which qualities they think they have. Invite questions from the whole class afterwards.

Activity 14   Game — five minutes

Activity 15   What mediation can and cannot do — 15 minutes

In pairs using the examples on Worksheet 3 overleaf think of one situation where mediation could not work and one where it could, with reasons why. Ask for reports back to the whole group and write them down as role-play scenarios to be used later.

Worksheet 3   What helps and hinders mediation (source: Lloyd 2000)

What helps:

- disputants have volunteered
- both want to find a solution and be in control of the outcome
- there is no great difference in power between them
- it can be done quickly; there is confidentiality
- both sides have the chance to let off steam
- they are prepared to let the mediator help them communicate with each other
- they can't find a solution but want to settle; other options aren't as good as mediation
- the personal safety of either party is not dependent on the outcome
- both see the mediator as impartial
- the issues can be resolved by the parties themselves.

What hinders:

- a great imbalance of power between the disputants
- a higher authority judgement is required
- legal action is already being carried out
- basic rights are at stake such as personal safety
- the parties are unwilling to participate
- one or both or the mediator feels unsafe
- neither party is able or willing to negotiate
- positions on both sides are extreme and have hardened.

Activity 16   Game — five minutes

Activity 17   Conflict management styles — 25 minutes

Explain that different people use different strategies for managing conflicts. These are learned in childhood and seem automatic and part of people's personalities. Some seem helpful but are not and can be unlearned and changed to more useful strategies. Our two main concerns when involved in a conflict are:

1. Achieving our own personal goals that conflict with another's. Your goal may be very important or not that important to you.
2. Keeping a good relationship with the other person. This relationship may be very important or not that important to you.

Divide the group into threes and ask them to tell each other what their conflict management styles are according to Handout 3 (see Appendix 5) and which one (if any) they would like to change it to and why. Also ask them to discuss if there is no change why not? Alternatively ask them to think of characters from soap operas that fit the descriptions and why. Afterwards have reports back to the whole group.

Activity 18   Game — five minutes

Activity 19   Destructive and constructive responses to conflict — 20 minutes

Divide the group into twos or threes and give out the examples on Worksheet 4 in the box opposite. Ask them to think of a typical school conflict they could be involved in as disputants and indicate in the middle on a scale of 1 (destructive) to 5 (constructive) how far they as a disputant would lean to destructive or constructive responses to the conflict.

Then ask for reports back to the whole group.

> **Worksheet 4**
> **Destructive and constructive responses to conflict** (source: Lloyd 2000)
>
> | DESTRUCTIVE | CONSTRUCTIVE |
> |---|---|
> | Smouldering | Letting off steam |
> | Fanning the flames | Cooling down |
> | Stoking the fire | Building bridges |
> | The blaze | Getting together |
> | The explosion | Working on the problem |
> | Counting the cost | Settling |
> | Repairing the damage | Preparing for the future |

Activity 20 Finish with a closing circle (see Chapter 4) — five minutes

Day 2 (six hours)

Materials
Active listening skills sheet, ground rules from day 1.

Aims of the session
- Introduce more mediation skills and techniques.
- Participants understand the nature of conflict and how to respond constructively.
- Practise mediation skills in groups.
- Participants learn more games.

Activity 1 Opening circle — five minutes (see Chapter 4)

Activity 2 Name game two — five minutes (see Chapter 4)

Activity 3 Refresher from first day — ten minutes
Using a flip chart ask participants to identify the different aspects covered on day 1. Try to cover as many of the following as possible: confidentiality, active listening, handling emotions; affirmations; negotiation, skills and qualities of a mediator: helpful and unhelpful circumstances; impartiality and hearing two sides; empathy; what mediation can and can't do; conflict management styles; destructive and constructive conflict.

Activity 4 Active listening to separate facts and feelings — 30 minutes
Explain how in conflicts people often get confused about what are the facts and what are their feelings. Strong feelings stop us from seeing the facts clearly. They also stop us from thinking clearly and cloud our judgement so we find it hard to make rational decisions. Feelings and emotions therefore need to be dealt with in a mediation session to enable disputants to think and decide rationally. We all react to situations differently and our reactions are usually based on past experiences or how we were brought up to think. It is very important for mediators to separate facts from feelings, and acknowledge and reflect them back to the disputants calmly.

Divide into threes and number each student 1, 2 and 3.

1 tells a real story of a time they had a strong feeling (such as excited, happy, angry or sad) about an event such as going on holiday or losing something. The trainer should give an example.

2 listens to the facts.

3 listens to the feelings.

2 reports back on the facts and 3 the feelings and 1 says whether they are accurate about each.

2 tells a story.

3 listens to the facts.

1 listens to the feelings.

3 reports back on the facts and 1 the feelings and 2 says whether they are accurate about each.

3 tells a story.

1 listens to the facts.

2 listens to the feelings.

1 reports back on the facts and 2 the feelings and 3 says whether they are accurate about each.

Ask for feedback from the class on which was easiest and most difficult: facts or feelings, to listen to or report back.

Activity 5   Game — five minutes

Activity 6   More on facts and feelings — ten minutes

Ask the group to name some of the emotions people feel when in conflict (such as anger, stress, hurt, annoyance, irritation, fury, rage, indifference, distrust, paranoia and impatience). Explain that these emotions are very real and although someone else might think a person is overreacting to the person concerned their emotional reaction is fully justified. The mediator needs to ensure that each disputant has a chance to say how he or she is feeling. If they do not say it directly they will say it indirectly and show it in their body language. Mediators need to spot these signs and reflect back that the disputant sounds or looks as if they are feeling a particular emotion. This gives them a chance to let off steam. Both should be given this opportunity in turn and both asked if they understand how the other one feels. Balance is also important when listening and responding to facts and feelings. The mediator needs to balance the need to move into problem solving and the speakers' need to give the full story and express all their feelings.

Activity 7   Getting ready to mediate — attentive body language — 20 minutes

Explain how mediators can show their interest non-verbally by using a combination of the following shown in Worksheet 5 opposite.

Worksheet 5　　　**Attentive body language**

Attentive body language includes:
◗ Open body posture
◗ Appropriate physical closeness
◗ Eye contact
◗ Affirmative gestures
◗ Stillness
◗ Animation

Ask the students to discuss what they understand these to mean and are there any others to add. Divide the group into threes. They take it in turns to talk briefly about something that interests them while the other two use the non-verbal behaviours to demonstrate interest.

Discussion with the whole class:
◗ How do you feel when you are using these behaviours?
◗ Do people acting as speakers feel that the non-verbal behaviours show interest and attention?
◗ When might you find it hard to show interest and attention like this?
◗ Can you identify any verbal or non-verbal behaviours which are used by people from various cultures?
◗ How can we ensure we are listening appropriately when mediating people from various cultures different to our own?

Activity 8　　Game — five minutes

Break — 15 minutes

Activity 9　　Building rapport — helpful and unhelpful behaviour — 25 minutes

Give out the questionnaire in Handout 4 (see Appendix 5) to each student for him or her to fill in. When finished, in pairs they tell each other they are doing well and what they need to improve.

Activity 10　Game — five minutes

Activity 11　Communication blockers — ten minutes

Explain that it is not useful for mediators to:

Order: 'You must', 'Don't do that'.

Threaten; 'You had better stop interrupting or else'.

Preach: 'You should'.

Lecture: 'Here is where you are getting it wrong'.

Judge: 'You don't seem to care very much'.

Excuse: 'Don't worry you'll feel better later'.

Analyse: 'I believe you haven't been able to admit this to yourself'.

Interrogate: 'What were you doing there? Who else was there? How long for?'.

Moralize: 'This is not really the sort of thing we like to hear about'.

In pairs take it in turns three minutes each way to tell your partner when any of the above have happened to you, how you felt and what you did well.

Activity 12   More on building rapport – 15 minutes

In threes sort out the examples on Worksheet 6 into helpful and unhelpful behaviours and then choose one of each and work out a short role play to illustrate each one. One person is the mediator and the other two disputants.

Worksheet 6 Active listening

Which types of behaviour are helpful and unhelpful? (source: Lloyd 2000)

Being honest about your own feelings	Being clear about your own role
Using judgemental statements	Ensuring they understand your role
Showing a balance of emotions and reason	Consistency
Offering interpretations of behaviour	Adopting a superior approach
Checking out how people are, the pace is right and so on	Using jargon or inappropriate language
	Reassurances about confidentiality
Pushing the pace	Interrupting
Showing respect	Realism
Openness	Not taking sides
Warmth	Equal access, time and space
Giving accurate feedback	Telling people what to do
Forgetting what people say and what is important to them	Not blaming

---

Activity 13   Demonstration of role plays showing helpful and unhelpful behaviour – ten minutes

After each role play invite comments from the class.

Lunch – one hour

Activity 14   Setting up mediation practice – 15 minutes

Divide the group into fours for them to build on their role plays this morning to invent a conflict between two of them to be mediated by the other two in a full mediation session. Give them prompt sheets (Handout 5, Appendix 5) as guidelines. If necessary give them pre-written conflict and role play situations (Handout 6, Appendix 5).

Activity 15   Demonstrations of full mediation sessions – 40 minutes

Ask half of the groups to demonstrate with prompt sheets or cards to help. After each one feed back from the class on what mediators did well and what they could have done better.

Activity 16   Game – five minutes

Activity 17   The rest of the demonstrations with feedback – 40 minutes

Ask the whole group for feedback on how well they did, and what was hard and easy.

Activity 18   Closing circle – five minutes

Day 3 (six hours)

Materials
Notepads and pen/pencil, course questionnaires, 14 sheets of A4, felt tip pens.

Aims of the session
- Introduce more mediation skills.
- More mediation practice.
- An understanding of the importance of identity, culture and backgrounds and the nature of stereotyping and prejudice.
- Plan peer mediation service and staff support.
- Learn more games.
- Evaluate effect of the course so far.

Activity 1   Opening circle — five minutes
Ask each person to name her or his favourite game either now or in the past.

Activity 2   Game: Falling game — five minutes (see Chapter 4)

Activity 3   Outline plan for the day and refresher from days 1 and 2 — 10 minutes
Recap confidentiality, and listening and mediation skills using flip chart notes from day 2 refresher activity and ask participants to identify the different aspects covered on day 2 (understanding conflict; separating facts and feelings; non-verbal communication between cultures; mediation practice; communication blockers; questionnaire - do people trust you?; building rapport – helpful and unhelpful behaviour).

Activity 4   Summarizing — five minutes
Explain that summarizing consists of several statements where the mediator sums up the disputant's feelings and the main points s/he has made. This shows the mediator has really grasped what s/he's been told and gives the disputant a chance to correct her if s/he has not. The next topic will be followed by an exercise in summarizing.

Activity 5   Taking pride in identity, culture and backgrounds and awareness raising on stereotypes, prejudice, bullying, sexism, racism and able-bodyism — 20 minutes
Talk about how our identities are made up of many features such as: our gender; age; talents; places we come from; culture; social class; abilities; and jobs we do. We are unique, yet also have features in common with others. Explain how people are often targeted and made to feel ashamed of aspects of their identity, especially unchangeable ones, such as disabilities, racial origin and gender but also aspects they can change like music tastes and hobbies. Therefore it is important to be proud of our identities, backgrounds and preferences. Ask them to quick-think (see Chapter 4) identities that get targeted and write on the flipchart. Ensure race, nationality, where they live, culture, social class, religion, ability and sexuality are included as well as physical abilities, characteristics, clothes, music tastes and interests. Explain how the targeting originates from outside the group and then becomes internalized within it and within each person in the group using the diagrams in Chapter 5.

Activity 6   Exploring diversity — 15 minutes

The trainer asks for a few volunteers to reflect the diversity in the group if possible. S/he listens to them talk in front of the class on the aspects of their identities, culture and family background focusing on what they are proud of. S/he asks them to choose one aspect they feel especially proud of and also something they never again want to hear said against that group. The trainer summarizes to the speaker the feelings they expressed and what s/he said, for them to have a chance to agree or disagree.

Divide the group into pairs with someone they do not usually pair up with to take turns two minutes each. They are to talk about all the identities they have (for example, female, white, Welsh, clever at maths, from single parent family, dancer) and which ones they are most proud of and what they never want to hear said about them. After each session the listener summarizes to the talker the main points of what s/he has said and felt.

Activity 7   Speakouts — 25 minutes

The rest of the group each take a turn in front of the group for about one minute speaking out about their identities and what they never want to hear said again about a particular group. For example they might refer to racist jokes about black people; young people being called 'yobs'; or blonde jokes about fair-haired girls.

Break — 15 minutes

Activity 8   Game: Prisoner — five minutes (see Chapter 4)

Activity 9   Five stages in mediation — five minutes

Summarize the five stages of the mediation process as follows:

1. Setting the scene.
2. Hearing the facts of the issues.
3. Exploring the issues and the feelings involved.
4. Building agreements.
5. Closure and follow-up.

Explain this is a general guide to help with structuring the session but mediators need to think quickly and flexibly, as sometimes it doesn't follow that order. For example stage 2 may be skipped with one of the disputants entering stage 3 immediately by bursting into tears. This emotional release will need to be encouraged fully before the disputants can move back to stage 2 to think and talk clearly about the facts of the problem and then to stage 3 to explore the feelings again before moving on to stage 4 to start thinking of solutions. Having done that the client may need to move back to stage 2, talk about the feelings and release more emotions connected to the actions s/he is planning.

Activity 10   Rehearsal of setting up role play mediation sessions — five minutes

Sessions in school will involve two mediators and two disputants who will have up to 30 minutes in each session depending on the time constraints in school. The session will have a clear beginning, middle and end though not necessarily of equal length. Peer mediators need to:

● Prepare the room and chairs beforehand to ensure privacy and no interruptions.

● Introduce themselves to the disputants, try to set them at ease and say how long the session can last.

- Explain confidentiality, the ground rules and the possibility of referral.

- Make sure all agree to conditions, including mediators.

- Go through each of the five stages of mediation using prompt sheets or cards to help. Let the disputants talk and listen well. Ensure the disputants state how the conflict made them feel emotionally. This is a 'detective' process so ask questions to clarify what is going on.

- Get disputants to sign the Commitment to Action form (see example in the box below) and read their solutions out loud.

- Finish by asking whether the disputants want another session and arrange it if necessary

- Give validations to the disputants throughout the mediation and especially at the end of the session.

Commitment to action form

I (name) agree to do the following from this moment onwards:

Signed ....

Activity 11   Summarizing the components of a mediation session – ten minutes

Quick-think the following on a flip chart, for example: ground rules, active listening skills, validations, empathy, emotional discharge, varied questions, summarizing, confidentiality, problem solving and the setting up and structure of the session.

Activity 12   Preparation for mediation role plays – ten minutes

Organize the students into the same groups as day 2 but this time they swap so a different couple practise mediating and the other pair are disputants. This is important for practice and assessment of each person's suitability as a mediator. See Appendix 5, Handout 6 for examples of role plays, but it is best for students and staff to use real situations and issues especially relevant to their school. Include as wide a variety of issues as possible. Either prepare these earlier or the students work out their role play just before their turn or as they are doing it. Remind them about confidentiality. Give out two role plays to each pair randomly and ask if they want to swap them around or make up their own. One pair can swap role-plays with another pair if they did it on day 2 or if they would feel more comfortable with a different scenario.

Activity 13   Practise role plays for the afternoon session – 15 minutes

Lunch – one hour

Activity 14   Role plays – 40 minutes

Proceed as on day 2.

Activity 15   Game – five minutes (see page Chapter 4).

Activity 16   Role plays – 40 minutes

Activity 17   Plan peer mediation programme – 30 minutes

- Explain the role of the staff supervisors and the administrative systems and recording forms that will be needed to run a mediation service.
- Think and listens with a scribe (see Chapter 4) to address the following questions:
  1. What form will the service take – Referrals with appointments? Drop-in-service? Both?
  2. Venue for mediation sessions?
  3. Name for your service? (see suggestions in Worksheet 7 below).
  4. What role could non-mediators play in the service?
  5. When can supervision meetings with teacher/s take place?
  6. Publicity?
- Decisions on dates and next steps towards setting up the service.
- Give out monitoring sheets (see Appendix 4) and explain how to fill in

---

Worksheet 7 What can you call your project?

Here are examples of names adopted by various peer mediation projects:
- Student Mediation Service
- Conflict Helpline 2004
- PMP (Peer Mediation Project)
- Conflict Resolution Scheme
- PALS (Pupils Always Listening Scheme)
- EAR4U
- Guardian Angels

Activity 18   Appreciations on backs – 20 minutes (see Chapter 4)

Activity 19   Course evaluations – five minutes (see Appendix 4)

Activity 20   Closing circle – five minutes

Ensure the group has arranged for a follow-up supervision session with their adult supervisor(s), then each person says one highlight from the three days and what the trainer/s did well.

Day 4 (three hours)

Aims of the session
- Discuss progress so far.
- Further mediation training.
- Dealing with difficult situations during mediation sessions.
- Relationship counselling.
- Future planning.
- Monitoring.
- End of training evaluation.

- Signing of contracts.
- Certificates.

Activity 1   Opening circle — five minutes

Activity 2   Plan for the session — five minutes
- Practise active listening.
- Discuss progress as mediators so far and troubleshoot if necessary.
- Learn relationship counselling as a form of mediation.
- Think about your next steps in the peer mediation service.

Activity 3   Active listening in pairs — ten minutes
The participants tell each other what's been enjoyable/easy as peer mediators and what's been difficult.

Activity 4   Game: the keys game — five minutes (see Chapter 4)

Activity 5   Discuss progress so far — 15 minutes
Ask the pairs of students to explain what they've been doing so far as mediators. Each pair talks about their activities. Iron out any problems.

Activity 6   Dealing with difficult situations during mediation sessions — 20 minutes
Divide the class into groups of four each with two disputants and two mediators. Distribute 'What to say in difficult situations', Handout 7 (see Appendix 5) among the groups so they can role-play each situation.

Activity 7   Role-play difficult situations — 20 minutes
Each group acts out one of the situations on Handout 6 (see Appendix 5) to illustrate how to respond to difficult situations.

Activity 8   Discussion on Activity 7 — five minutes

Activity 9   Game — five minutes

Break — five minutes

Activity 10   Relationship counselling — five minutes (see Chapter 5)
Briefly explain the process and its purpose and give out guide from Chapter 5.

Activity 11   Demonstrate with two people — ten minutes
Ask for two volunteers who want to get closer, improve their relationship and/or resolve past or current problems between them. Demonstrate the process with them.

Activity 12   Practise relationship counselling — 15 minutes
Divide the group into threes, name each person A, B or C.
A counsels B and C for five minutes.
B counsels A and C for five minutes.
C counsels A and B for five minutes.

Activity 13   Discussion — five minutes

Discuss the process of relationship counselling and plan how it can be used as part of the peer mediation service in school.

Activity 14   Game — five minutes

Activity 15   Monitoring and evaluation — 15 minutes

Ask each student to fill in monitoring sheets and end of course evaluation sheets and collect them in (see Appendix 4).

Activity 16   Each peer mediator signs a contract — five minutes (see example in Worksheet 8)

Worksheet 8   Peer mediator contract (source: Britton 2000)

I understand my role as peer mediator is to help students resolve conflicts peacefully. I will do my best to respect the disputants in mediation, remain neutral and keep the process confidential.

I agree to the following:
▶ To complete all training and attend all supervision and practice sessions unless I am ill.
▶ To maintain confidentiality in all mediation sessions.
▶ To perform all duties required of a peer mediator, including conducting mediation, completing monitoring forms and promoting the service.
▶ To maintain satisfactory school conduct, including asking for mediation before taking any action in conflicts I am involved in.
▶ To make up any work missed during training.
▶ To serve as a peer mediator until my last term at school.

If these responsibilities are not met the consequences are:
First time: Warning
Second time: No longer a peer mediator.

I accept these responsibilities until my last term in school.

Student signature

Date

Activity 17   Closing circle — five minutes

Each student appreciates their mediation partners and the trainer.

Finish — Give out certificates now or at a later date (see Chapter 5)

Chapter 7

Circle of Friends: a strategy to facilitate inclusion though peer support

 The only reward of virtue is virtue; the only way to have a friend is to be one.

(Ralph Waldo Emerson)

Taking care of each other in family and friendship circles has been the structure of human relationships throughout history, yet, in the developed world as wealth and mobility have increased, we are becoming increasingly isolated from one another. The Circle of Friends approach is one of many peer support strategies to restore and develop the basic human practice of group support and action to ensure that everyone is included in all levels of society.

The approach has been widely used with young people of varied ages and needs including those with autistic spectrum disorders (ASD) (Whitaker et al. 1998). Initially developed in Canada and the USA, Circle of Friends has been used extensively to help include students in mainstream schools (Perske 1988). Although there are many informal, effective and unobtrusive ways in which young people enable their peers to be included in the everyday life of schools, sometimes a more organized and structured approach such as Circle of Friends is needed. This problem-solving approach can enable a group of peers to help young people who are socially isolated for a variety of reasons by working with them on how to make and keep friends.

Colin Newton and Derek Wilson of Inclusive Solutions have written extensively on how to set up this approach and offer training courses.

'Circle of friends is an approach to enhancing the inclusion, in a mainstream setting, of any young person (known as "the focus child"), who is experiencing difficulties in school because of a disability, personal crisis or because of their challenging behaviour towards others.' (Newton and Wilson 2003).

As activists in the inclusion movement Newton and Wilson have developed their Circle of Friends model from the ideas and work of several worldwide organizations and institutions devoted to developing inclusive practices. These include: Jack Pearpoint and Marsha Forest; the UK-based campaigning group, The Alliance for Inclusive Education; and the pioneering work of Richard Rieser and Micheline Mason of Disability Equality in Education (DEE) set up in 1996.

The rationale

Newton and Wilson on their website, www.inclusive-solutions.com, advocate full inclusion for all including 'the belief that there is no social justice until each belongs and has an equal place in our schools and communities'.

This idea of inclusion underpins the Circle of Friends approach advocated by Newton et al. (1996). They describe their model as simply recognizing that someone who shows distressed and difficult behaviour is likely to be isolated from their peer group. Such young people are usually described as 'having no friends', 'unable to make or sustain relationships', 'always fighting or arguing with others'. Less kind descriptions are 'a nutter', 'mad', 'always getting in trouble for something'.

Studies on the process of circular causation are cited by Newton et al. (1996) in their account of a vicious circle of isolation and antisocial behaviour. Once young people internalize the idea of their unpopularity and experience others' enjoyment in provoking them, they easily conclude that they have nothing to lose by acting out their despair and bad feelings in further antisocial behaviour. The subsequent reactions of the others confirm the isolated youngster's worst fears about her/himself and how others see her/him. This vicious circle ensures that the effects of an isolated young person's antisocial behaviour become the subsequent cause of its perpetuation.

This process is often accelerated by the adults involved and their interventions or non-interventions. Some behaviour policies can advocate ignoring difficult behaviour in the belief that it could be reinforced by the reward of attention. These policies give out messages from the adults that students should not get involved with difficult students and should ignore them. Furthermore the exclusion message is reinforced when these difficult students are sent out of class to 'Time Out' rooms. Although this is helpful for saving the face of a young person and limiting her/his audience it is unlikely to address the unmet needs that cause the behaviour.

The Circle of Friends approach is at the opposite end of the spectrum of interventions from those that ignore difficult behaviour. It a systemic approach acknowledging the power of the peer group and pupil culture to be a positive as well as a negative influence on individual behaviour. If peer group isolation can worsen things for a distressed student then it follows that increasing that individual's inclusion within his/her peer group could help. A vicious circle can become virtuous in the right conditions and context.

For schools the resource implications of this approach are minimal. It does not involve a major commitment of time from staff apart from the time needed to set up the friendship circle and a member of staff to facilitate its problem-solving skills as it develops. This is because the key resources, other young people, are already there and they, rather than the adults, do the true work. The adult's role is to meet with the circle and the focus child for about half an hour weekly to facilitate their problem solving in the early stages. From then on the circle is mostly self-sustained and providing support for the focus child without too much regular adult input. With careful planning and reliable adult commitment positive results materialize quickly.

Different models of Circle of Friends

There are three types of Circle of Friends that vary according to the extent to which those participating know the identity of the focus young person and how many of the group or class participates.

1. *Highly focused Circle of Friends*. This involves a small number of selected peers who meet regularly with the explicit purpose of helping a named young person who is not present at the initial discussion. This is the most widely adopted approach in schools. It is important that the focus young person and their parents are happy with the approach before it is started. Full details of how to set up this approach can be found in Newton et al. (1996) and Taylor (1996). Whitaker et al. (1998) carried out an evaluation of several circles of friends involving pupils with ASD conducted in this way. They found that if the child with ASD became the centre of attention this could lead to 'increased egocentricity'. However, their social integration improved, and there was a higher level of peer contact, reduced anxiety and improved behaviour. In addition there were benefits for the other circle participants such as enhanced self-esteem.

2. *Circle of Friends with the focus young person present but anonymous*. This is the same as the model above except that the young person is present at the initial discussion session though not identified. It is explained to all participants that the circle is for the children to get to know about how to be good friends. For more details see Shotton (1998).

3. *Several Circles of Friends in one class*. This is based on a wider community of support for the focus young person often to the whole class. In this approach several circles are set up in the class so that all members are part of a circle where the same issues are explored. This means that all class members, including the focus young person, learn about friendship and so hopefully develop skills to help them include more socially isolated or challenging students so no one feels excluded. See Barrett and Randall (2001) for details.

Steps for setting up and leading a Circle of Friends

What follows is a guideline based on the 'Highly focused Circle of Friends' model. Fuller descriptions can be found in Newton and Wilson (2003) and Whitaker et al. (1998).

1. *Get permission for involvement from school staff.*
   Schools already promoting a supportive ethos are likely to be sympathetic to both the purpose and the process, providing they are explained clearly. See the box overleaf.

An introduction to Circles of Friends - a staff guide
(source: Whitaker et al. 1998)

These brief notes will give you some background information and an idea of what would be entailed in setting up and running a Circle of Friends in your school:

1. Circles of Friends originated in North America as one of a range of strategies to encourage the inclusion of children with disabilities into mainstream settings. Circles have been used to support children with a wide range of disabilities and have also been used in the community.

2. A circle usually consists of between six and eight volunteers (most often from the same class or tutor group) who meet regularly (usually weekly) with the 'focus child' and an adult. The circle has three main tasks: to offer encouragement and recognition for successes and progress; to identify difficulties, set targets and devise strategies for achieving targets; and to help put these ideas into practice.

3. Setting up a circle includes the following steps:
   ◗ Gaining the support and agreement of the focus child and his or her parents.
   ◗ A meeting with the whole class (which the focus child does not attend) aimed at recruiting volunteers, which takes roughly 30–40 minutes.
   ◗ Informing the parents of volunteers and gaining their agreement to their children's participation.
   ◗ Weekly meetings of the circle, the focus child and an adult facilitator (taking 20–30 minutes).

2. *Talk to the parents of the focus child.*

Parents need to know clearly what is entailed and the possible outcomes. They need to have a realistic idea about the term 'Circle of Friends' and accept that friendships cannot simply be created by it in the same way as they would informally. In the Leicester project for students with autism, Whitaker et al. (1998) asked parents whether or not their children knew of their own diagnosis, whether the school knew it and, if so, whether the label could be mentioned in any discussions. They found that it was possible to run a circle without the label and the peer groups consistently demonstrated 'considerable perception about the nature of the child's difficulties'. They suggested the information sheet opposite.

3. *Discuss the idea with the focus young person.*

Explain the process and find out whether s/he would like to try it. Whitaker et al. (1996) remind us that 'careful (and subjective) judgement' is required for a circle to have the necessary free and informed consent of the focus student. The young person's agreement should be based on information made as accessible as possible. Agreement or refusal by the child must not be based on misleading ideas on what the circle can offer and how they will feel in the process. If the young person agrees, ascertain whether s/he wants to be present at the initial discussion with the group concerned so that s/he has the option to be there. If s/he chooses not to be present arrange to tell her/him afterwards what the group talked about.

An introduction to Circles of Friends – a parents' guide
(source: Whitaker et al. 1996)

1. What is a 'Circle of Friends'?

   A circle is a group of between six and eight youngsters who have volunteered to meet regularly with your child and a teacher (usually this is for 20–30 minutes per week).

2. What is a circle for and what happens?

   The circle has four main aims:
   - to create a support network for your child
   - to provide your child with encouragement and recognition for any achievements and progress
   - to work with your child in identifying difficulties and coming up with practical ideas to help sort out these difficulties
   - to help put these ideas into practice.

The adult is there to help the circle, but the work is done by the youngsters with your child coming up with ideas, trying things out and reporting back.

The circle cannot provide instant friendship but we hope that it will help your child to build closer and better relationships with other children.

3. How will it be set up?

   The members of your child's class would be asked if they are interested in volunteering to be in the circle. Your child's teacher will explain to them what this involves – usually this is best done when your child is not actually in the room.

We almost always end up with more volunteers than we need and your child's class teacher will carry out the selection. The group then meets regularly with an adult.

4. Will it help?

   Obviously we can't guarantee this. However, Circles of Friends have been used quite widely in North America and are increasingly being used in this country. As far as we know, Leicestershire was the first local education authority to use them and evaluations of that project were very positive indeed:
   - children at the centre of the circles have shown improved behaviour and less worry about mixing with their classmates
   - the volunteers have been very good at coming up with creative and practical ideas.
   - most volunteers have been keen to continue their involvement
   - school staff have found them very worthwhile.

Please contact .... if you would like to discuss 'Circles' in more detail or if you have any questions or concerns.

FAQS (adapted from: Newton and Wilson 2003)

'What would you do with a child that smells, surely you couldn't build a circle for them?'
Build a Circle of Friends! Friends are people who care enough to notice and tell the truth.
Ask yourself; 'Who would tell you if you smelled?', 'Who would you be angry with for not
telling you?', 'Who could you bear to hear this news from?'. Personalizing the issue makes it
easier to think what you might do and generate ideas for what could be done for the focus
child. Remember that the person who smells bad may be aware of this but is unable to ask
for help to overcome the problem. A 'Circle of Friends' provides a context in which help can
be sought.

4. *Hold an initial discussion with the focus student's class or group.*
    The agenda outlined here is based on Newton et al. (1996). According to Whitaker et
    al. (1996) the meeting in its own right is powerful and can make a huge impact on
    the group members' attitudes to the focus child, regardless of whether a circle is
    established afterwards. This first session needs about an hour in which the adult
    establishes a spirit of shared responsibility. It is best for an adult unfamiliar to the
    group to lead this initial meeting, with the key teacher there. This encourages a new
    perspective on the situation and changes the dynamic. Explain that the aim of the
    meeting is to form a Circle of Friends and to recruit participants. Highlight the
    special nature of the discussion and how it is unusual to talk about someone behind
    their back but the focus young person had agreed because the purpose was to help
    him/her. Talk about confidentiality and stress how much they could help the focus
    young person. Give three ground rules: listen to each other as one person speaks at a
    time; respect each other's thoughts and feelings with no put-downs; and keep
    confidentiality. Ask them to voice their opinions on the following and write up
    comments on a flip chart:

    a) what they have liked about the focus person's behaviour in the past;
    b) what they have found difficult about her/his behaviour;
    c) how they would feel if they had few or no friends;
    d) how they would behave if they had few or no friends;
    e) suggest ideas for helping the focus person (for example, one or two of them hang
        out with him/her at lunchtime; one of them sits next to her/him at lectures/work;
        ask him/her to join in social activities; ask him/her if they can help with his/her
        work; help him/her give up any addictions to harmful substances like cigarettes
        or alcohol; sugar; help him/her eat more sensibly; if s/he starts getting wound up
        calm her/him down or listen to him sound off privately; validate her/him; get
        her/his attention on to positive ideas.

FAQS (adapted from: Newton and Wilson 2003)

'How long do children need to remain as members of a circle?'
Time boundaries are important and prospective circle members should know that their
commitment will be expected for a set period (for example, six weeks, a school term or half
term). After this they will have the choice of continuing for a further period or of opting out
for a while.

Now ask for volunteers to become a Circle of Friends for the focus person. Explain what would be required such as a lunchtime meeting once a week. Inform them that only about six can be chosen initially but that new people may be needed in the circle at a later date. Stress that they can leave at any point. Also tell them if they are not chosen now they can still take responsibility for helping and that a letter home will be sent to all volunteers' parents asking for consent. Distribute small pieces of paper and ask them to write their names on the paper with either a yes or a no. Remind them about confidentiality and that there is no pressure to write yes.

Select six to eight young people as much at random as possible while ensuring a balance of very able students and those who have some difficulties. Arrange the first circle meeting as soon as possible. Newton and Wilson (2003) suggest the following options for choosing circle members:

- Random selection. The facilitator can be blindfolded or close their eyes and point at volunteers randomly until the required number are selected or names can be picked from a hat.

- Student selection. The class nominates students who they feel are best suited to support the focus student. They can consider shared interests, hobbies and activities or qualities such as strong personality, communication skills, negotiation skills, popularity and street credibility.

- Compromise selection involving facilitator, teacher and students. The facilitator chooses two students on the basis of their contribution to the discussion. The teacher chooses a further two members on the basis of his or her knowledge of the class and the students choose the rest.

- The focus student selects members of his or her circle from volunteers. S/he would be given the names of volunteers and asked to suggest other names of students who would be helpful, supportive and usefully challenging. This would provide maximum control to the focus student but the possible loss of the security and clear boundaries s/he would have meeting an already formed circle of volunteers.

FAQS (adapted from: Newton and Wilson 2003)

'What if, at the end of the whole-class session, no one shows a willingness to be part of the focus child's circle?'
Put the issue back to the class by asking, 'Is there anyone who people think would be a helpful member of the circle and who hasn't yet come forward?'. Groups always have suggestions when asked this and they are usually the right ones. The individuals nominated in this way usually agree!

5. *Consult the parents of circle members.*
   Provide information to the parents of volunteers and seeking their consent is important if the circle is run by outside agencies. Usually the best method is a standard letter sent to the parents giving some background information and inviting them to contact the headteacher with any concerns or questions. Consent is presumed if the parents do not reply.

> **FAQS** (adapted from: Newton and Wilson 2003)
>
> 'What if a disclosure is made during the circle meeting?'
> When briefing a new Circle of Friends ensure that all realize the meaning of confidentiality and the requirements of the Children Act (see Chapter 9). They must be reminded that if they hear something serious about or from the focus student that they should speak to an adult.

6. *First circle meeting.*

   The six to eight volunteers and the focus young person attend this and subsequent meetings. This meeting starts the process of building relationships between the circle and the focus student. It is important to mobilize the circle's motivation to help and to ensure the focus child hears the others acknowledge his or her strengths as well as the difficulties which s/he needs to work on. They all need to share responsibility towards the goal of helping the focus student deal more effectively with everyday situations. A typical agenda could be:

   ● Open with a fun warm-up game (see Chapter 5).

   ● Remind the group about the ground rules.

   ● Each person says why he or she wants to help the focus student.

   ● Ask the group to list positive points about the focus student (point out that s/he didn't hear what was said at the first session). Ask the focus student to add any to list.

   ● Each person gives their key ideas on what the focus student needs to work on while the adult writes them up as a list. These should include specific descriptions of behaviours.

   ● Ask the group to turn every problem behaviour pattern into a positive target (describing what the focus student should be doing rather than not doing).

   ● Ask the focus student to add to any of the lists above.

   ● Introduce problem solving by explaining the need to work on one or two targets at a time and ask the group including the focus student to decide which target(s). Suggest starting with something quickly achievable.

   ● A quick-think (see Chapter 5) on possible ways to get to the target, select jointly and help group spell out steps.

   ● The group is to agree responsibilities and boundaries and decisions on who is doing what (emphasize that the focus student is responsible for own behaviour).

   ● Emphasize realism about speed of change and setbacks.

   ● Group discussion about what would be different if the focus student achieved these targets.

   ● A fun activity to end with everyone agreeing the name for the group.

The adults' role is to facilitate rather than control this process. If the participants are to assume maximum responsibility and co-operate creatively, adults will need to hold back or be discreet when they feel the instinct to teach, direct and protect. However, Whitaker et al. (1996) emphasize that the adult must be prepared to step in with guidance when necessary at any point in the process. The adult retains responsibility and authority for determining the overall boundaries and direction of the circle and for the well-being of the participants.

This may entail teaching skills such as providing constructive criticism (see Chapter 8). It also requires the provision of personal support for individuals having to deal with their own and others' strong negative reactions and emotions; and sometimes taking control if the process takes unhelpful directions such as some members dominating others or the goals of the circle being ignored.

FAQS (adapted from: Newton and Wilson 2003)

'Can circles co-opt members?'
Yes. Stronger, older peers, relations, or even adults may at times be usefully co-opted into the circle and strengthen its work. Diversity brings strength and this is at the root of circle work. The right people who can make a difference to the individual need to be present. Sometimes the right person is the one who is giving the circle most concerns because of their antagonism towards the focus student. A constructive approach to this antagonism is to say that this student also has an unmet need to belong and co-opting him or her is a step towards meeting this need and could deal with the antagonism at the same time.

7. *Ongoing circle meetings.*
    Circle meetings should probably be held weekly perhaps over a minimum of six weeks. However, they may be more frequent than this and over a term or more. The frequency should be tailored to the participants' requirements. Topics such as, 'what makes a good friend', 'emotions', 'bullying', 'assertiveness' and many more can be covered. It is important that the young people involved can bring the issues concerning them to the circle meetings. Circles would be lead by the adult who should be constant and someone who everyone is comfortable speaking with. A plan outlining what will happen within each session may also be useful. Consideration should be given to which room is used and whether non-participating young people will be using this room at the same time. Following the use of Circle of Friends it would be important to evaluate outcomes against aims. The format of the circle should be tailored around the focus young person. It may be best to keep this simple with an informal chat about issues for the focus young person or the participants during which the group identify ways they will help her/him and reflect upon how previous help has gone. However, it may be felt that the sessions would benefit from more structure and built-in fun elements. A possible structure for a session could be as follows:

    ● Open with a fun warm up game.
    ● Remind the group about the ground rules.
    ● Review what has gone well regarding helping the focus person including all the participants' achievements as well as those of the focus person.
    ● Discuss the difficulties that have arisen, including when and where they happened and possible reasons for them.
    ● Generate ideas for dealing with the difficulties and decide who will do what.
    ● Each person speak in a round on a topic connected to the above, such as bullying.
    ● Group discussion (key element) to include talk about ways the circle members could help each other in connection with the topic.
    ● Close with a fun activity.

Not all these sections need be covered in each session and careful consideration of the appropriate length of the session should be made to maximize its effectiveness.

FAQS (adapted from: Newton and Wilson 2003)

'What about Circle members who become over enthusiastic?'
Circle members who are very enthusiastic to support, befriend and bring about change in the focus student can be very endearing to the facilitator. However, some pitfalls are disappointment, over zealous watchfulness, inability to cope with the focus child's needs or being vulnerable to bullying, violent outbursts. Careful support, encouragement and guidance are needed from the adult and honest discussion with circle members about the issue. Individuals should be encouraged to work together and to avoid situations where they may become vulnerable. Having more than one circle member involved in every planned activity provides safety.

8. *Keeping up the momentum.*
   For some circle members helping the focus student is its own reward, and in the longer term hopefully the relationship becomes mutually supportive and rewarding. However, Whitaker et al. (1996) found that circle members can be demotivated if they feel they are doing all the giving and getting nothing back. They suggest the following strategies to mitigate against this possibility:

   - Recognition and encouragement for all circle members (including the focus student) for their efforts. Openly acknowledge any feelings that they are getting nowhere and/or they are receiving no thanks from the focus student. The circle's long term willingness to stick with the focus student can impart a vital message to her/him so that its impact is as powerful in the long run as any of the specific skills and strategies targeted.

   - Setting attainable targets, achieving them and seeing progress in the focus student are a major source of satisfaction. Although circles can set ambitious targets and manage to achieve them the adult may need to intervene to ensure they are realistic. They may need help negotiating with school staff to ensure that their strategies are acceptable and supported.

   - Meeting the circle members' need may involve the adult facilitator allowing the circle to evolve in its own way while keeping sight of the original aims. For example, it may become a mutual support group with members using it to resolve their own personal problems as well as those of the focus student. In fact the latter can be involved in the process of helping another circle member. Another example is when it may be appropriate for the circle to meet without the focus student especially if s/he is giving little back to the group or actively rejecting their attempts to help.

Important points about Circle of Friends

- The friends need reminding that they are not responsible for the focus person and/or her/his behaviour.
- The focus person may use being a member of the circle as a reward or threat to other young people. If this happens the circle need to talk about their group being voluntary and democratic and therefore not under the ownership of the focus person.
- The content of the meetings can vary greatly in terms of emotions expressed. The facilitator needs to maintain boundaries and ensure discussions feel safe for everyone.
- The process can enable all the participants to reflect on, express and come to terms with difficult feelings and experiences and to develop empathy for others.

9. *Ending the Circle of Friends*

   After six weeks the group may decide bi-weekly meetings are sufficient if enough progress has been made. Eventually they can decide to finish completely when the focus person and the rest of the group feel ready with the proviso of another meeting a few months later to review progress.

FAQS (adapted from: Newton and Wilson 2003)

'I can think of at least seven children in my class who would benefit from this approach. Should I run circles for each of them?'
A Circle of Friends with more than one focus child would be unmanageable, but a friendship circle could be effective. Sustaining relationships can be difficult for all students not just those labelled different or disabled. A group of between six and eight students having friendship difficulties could benefit from a programme of relationship building activities in 'friendship sessions' for about eight weeks.

Troubleshooting

Newton and Wilson (2003) list frequently asked questions and give their answers with the proviso that they cannot know what will work best in any particular context and urge readers to be creative. See the box below for an adaptation.

FAQS (adapted from: Newton and Wilson 2003)

'What other ways are there to encourage friendship?'
Just being with other children can be critical in the development of friendships for the most vulnerable especially those being educated in segregated settings. Mainstream classroom techniques to encourage friendships can include all the peer support systems outlined in this book. Schools can encourage disabled and able-bodied students to get involved with other children in extra-curricular activities, and assemblies and lessons focussing on friendship can be included in the school curriculum. Inducting new pupils is an excellent opportunity to teach friendship skills with a welcoming committee and/or buddies to help

the new student adapt. Teachers can arrange for students who need friends to work with more sociable classmates on various everyday activities.

'Can the circle meet without the focus student being present?'
Strictly speaking this is unethical as the circle is built around the focus student who must have the final say on decisions and the power to influence the perception of others. However, when things appear to be going badly some facilitators may need to convene a circle meeting without her/him present to give the others a chance to discharge some of their frustrations. This may be a helpful step to take if the alternative is the demise of the circle, but if there are frequent circle meetings without the focus student it is no longer a 'Circle of Friends'.

What if it all goes wrong?
A Circle of Friends involves risks but it can stop children been excluded so it is a risk worth taking. It is best to assess the risks within your own situation and to plan your action accordingly. Aim to work with another person and always ensure that the key stakeholders in your school fully understand and support your efforts. Never do this work in isolation. Particular risks include the following:

- Sabotage by senior members of staff or by colleagues as a result of chaotic planning, or from a lack of understanding of the process.
- Continuity breaks when meetings come to an untimely end due to cover problems, staff absence or the work not percieved as high priority. This breaks the flow and commitment of the circle and is particularly unhelpful to the focus student.
- Others feel excluded. Other staff or students may feel threatened and de-skilled by the relationship you have formed with the focus student and their circle. They may feel resentful of the time you have negotiated for your work with the circle. The associated behaviour patterns can be potentially destructive.
- Over enthusiasm by individual circle members can lead to their being in high-risk situations with the focus student. Individuals always need reminding to work together in mutual support rather than going it alone.
- Parental anxiety. Parents of the focus student or circle members may become unduly anxious about what is going on for their child. This usually occurs where parents have not been properly informed about what is happening or are relying on rumour, or reacting to a particular event.
- Over ambition in the circle's early planning and expectations of being able to make a difference. Things can often be brought back on track if you simplify and reduce the number of aims being worked towards. You will not get it right first time every time.

'What if...?'
Sometimes we have no idea what the way forward is. The culture of professionalism implies that every situation is covered and every question has an answer if only we knew to whom we should refer. However, it is more helpful to say with honesty that you do not know what to do next. It passes the power back to the person that is seeking help.

Stage 3
Making peer support work in the long term

Sustaining the programmes, supervision and child protection

Assessment, monitoring, evaluation and accreditation

They do it this way: examples of good practice in the long term

Chapter 8

Sustaining the programmes, supervision and child protection

 Light tomorrow with today.

(Elizabeth Barrett Browning)

Sustaining the programmes

How the service operates from day to day will play a large part in how well the service is sustained in the long term. Key elements in the successful operation of a peer support programme are:

- *Launch activities.* This is a public relations exercise involving all participants in the project preferably near the beginning of a school term. Communicating with the whole institution community and outside agencies will include all or any of: presentation of certificates, producing publicity material, websites, email addresses, letters to parents, students and staff, school assemblies, talks to tutor groups , newsletters, press releases, media involvement, and presentations to governors and important local community members.

- *Peer support policy document.* This is likely to be the original proposal updated after training and consultation. It can be included in other related policies such as those for behaviour or anti-bullying and it needs to state aims and objectives, and how it is organized, operated, financed and evaluated.

- *Ongoing publicity.* Ideally peer supporters will be appointed to their specific roles with rotas and supervision sessions organized for at least a term at a time. The key worker will need to ensure notes are sent out and that continual communication with relevant staff and target groups ensures they and peer supporters are kept informed.

Wolstanton High School follow-up training with Netta Cartwright

- *Regular staff supervision of peer supporters*. Ideally supervisors should meet peer supporters once a week or, at least once every two weeks, ensuring that peer supporters are not stretched beyond the boundaries of their competence. Regularity is the most important aspect and, if possible, such meetings should take place during the school day as part of morning tutor time periods.

- *Follow-up training*. As the programme unfolds opportunities for refresher or updating sessions will be helpful about once a term. This keeps the momentum going, irons out problems and adds further skills.

- *Follow-up activities*. Students can network with other peer supporters in their neighbourhood or further afield by taking part in events arranged by organizations like The Peer Mediation Network, Trust for the Study of Adolescence and Re-evaluation Counselling.

Students Youth Voice Peer Power event

- *Planning the next year's programme*. The training of the next cohort of peer supporters and supervising staff is best planned at least a term in advance to sustain the service. Some programmes involve the current peer supporters in the recruitment and interviewing processes. Once selected the next cohort of peer supporters could become apprentices learning 'on the job' with the older peer supporters. This would be before, during or after their training course depending on the school calendar. Issues around competition and possessiveness often occur at this point and it is best to address them openly in joint sessions with both groups and the key workers/supervisors.

Although there are common factors that lend themselves to sustainability there is no project that is exactly the same or that has the same outcomes. Peer support depends on facilitating systems like training, school policies and personnel each bringing with them complex values and assumptions. However, the experience of 35 schools in England that have used the co-counselling model over two decades has shown the possibility of long term projects being sustained. At least 31 of the 35 schools initiated in the co-counselling model (Cartwright 2005) are still running their own programmes led by the trained staff or staff they have subsequently trained. Of these 12 have been doing it for five years or more, 11 for three or four years and eight are in their first or second year of peer support (Cartwright 2005). In these schools Cartwright observed some key elements that promote sustainability of peer support systems. Some of these schools and others are featured as case studies in Chapter 10.

Key elements of sustainability (Cartwright 2005)

- support, commitment and direct involvement from senior management
- adequate funding and time resource
- quality training
- fully trained and supported staff co-ordinators
- careful selection of students
- maintaining the momentum
- networking and sharing experiences
- regular monitoring and evaluation.

Adequate time and funding resources

A basis for sustainability is adequate time allowed for peer support within the curriculum coupled with financial backing for at least two years, although some schools begin with sufficient funding for the first year only and find more later. Ideally training for students and staff takes place during school time as part of the curriculum. Although many schools run courses at lunchtimes, twilight time or at weekends this is not recommended for the basic training as it undermines the importance of the activity and can exclude many students as well as depending on the goodwill of staff. Those schools that are pressured for time tend to cut back on the amount they can allow for peer support and therefore limit its impact. As a headteacher of a primary school in Stafford explained,

'The only factor that has limited the success is time – or lack of it – in terms of the number of changes, initiatives and improvements we are choosing or being forced to make.

However, while we have not implemented all of the elements of this project as planned we have altered the culture of the way that pupils interact and as such this has been a success.'

The headteacher of Flegg High School, Norfolk maintains that schools must commit appropriate resources for peer support to succeed. He warns against the mistake of seeing peer support as an 'add-on, rather than as an integral part of the school's approach to the well-being of its pupils' (Moldrich and Carpentieri 2005).

Many organizations are now working with schools on a wide range of peer support projects and in many different ways. However, not all are given time and resources to be sustained in the long term. Baginsky (2001) examined peer support schemes in 14 schools where NSPCC were involved. The schools included in this study were provided with training and limited initial support but the schools were then expected to assume responsibility for its day to day functioning. In the longer term those schools able to invest this time and effort were able to sustain schemes. After 12 months it appeared, however, that only four of the 14 schemes examined were reasonably strong and seen to be succeeding by the teachers interviewed. Another four schemes were either 'limping along' or said to be in temporary intermission. This means that six schemes had effectively stopped, although a few teachers hoped that when more resources and/or staff time were available they may be revived.

Financial resources seem to be less of a problem once the initial outlay has been found. Sustaining the project afterwards is relatively inexpensive as the trained staff supervise and train each year's new cohort of peer supporters. Many schools finance projects from their own budgets and this kind of commitment motivates the sustaining of their system. However, local and national charities and government funds are often good sources of income when large sums are needed for joint projects. A study of 35 schools using the co-counselling model in England (Cartwright 2005) showed that 19 were self-funded and the rest funded by Barclays New Futures, and the Children's Fund. Six schools in Tamworth (Case study 4 in Chapter 10) could not have embarked on their joint project without the £6,000 grant from their headteachers' funds (Cartwright 2005).

Fully trained staff co-ordinators

Cartwright (2005) surveyed schools where peer support, using the co-counselling model, had been active for over three years. She found that eight schools' peer support schemes had been led by senior managers, four by teachers, four by learning mentors, three by heads of year, two by counsellors and one by a special educational needs co-ordinator. Nearly all had one other staff member or a small team to sustain the projects. They all had at least one motivated and adaptable person with enough non-contact time for the necessary but time consuming administrative work with contracts, memos, rotas and reminders for the peer supporters. This model entailed at least one member of staff regularly supervising the peer supporters and evaluating and monitoring their work. The co-ordinator registered the students' attendance at supervision meetings and their peer support activities. Although they liaise with other staff to ensure an efficient system, the co-ordinator may at times work on their own with only their training, enthusiasm and commitment to maintain their motivation. This can translate into isolation and, when there is lack of support from senior management long term, peer support is at risk of simply fizzling out. Another factor contributing to the demise of a service is when the co-ordinator leaves and is not replaced or when a person gets the job by default or is thrust into it without consultation or training. The headteacher of Flegg High School warns against 'the mistake of giving the programme to somebody because nobody else will do it' (Moldrich and Carpentieri 2005). This happened in two out of 35 schools surveyed by Cartwright (2005).

Careful selection and training of peer supporters

When deciding on the age of peer supporters most schools opt to train students who have one or two years left before they leave. This ensures there is enough time for them to work and establish themselves as peer supporters. Most secondary schools train some of Year 9 or Year 10 students and have a rolling programme. In the primary schools Year 4 and/or 5 students are trained. In middle schools Year 8 students are trained and in some schools Year 12 students are trained but this is becoming less popular with the increasing demands on post-16 students. How trainees are recruited and who determines the nature, scope and success of programmes is key (see Chapter 4). It is important that schools have a clear process for selection with sensitivity to the backgrounds of the students and a commitment to ensure that peer supporters reflect the student body, particularly in relation to gender, ethnicity, and physical and academic ability. Some schools use formal selection with application forms and interviews. Others use positive selection with peer and/or adult nominations to ensure a balance of gender, race, and physical and academic ability. Self-selection has been useful in the context of self-help around particular issues such as bereavement or bullying. Some schools train as many students as possible, for example small primary schools have trained whole year groups. Usually the type of service determines the number and nature of trainees. For example, in a school with sixth form entry at least 12 mentors were trained for each tutor group to have two mentors. At Longton High School (Case study 2 in Chapter 10) there was a need to positively discriminate in order to achieve an equal balance of ethnicity as part of the school's anti-racist strategies.

Individual programmes for individual schools

The key to long term success of peer support in a school is a programme designed to meet its own unique needs and its ability to evolve over time. Many schools observing the positive effect of peer support in other schools justifiably wish to adopt similar programmes. Problems can arise, however, if school staff rush into a scheme without tailoring it to their school's unique set of circumstances. One school may wish to focus on reducing bullying, another may aim to reduce exclusions and another to ease the transition from primary to secondary school. Childline warns schools against 'pre-packaged' peer support programmes and advocates the kind of 'freedom and flexibility' that their courses can provide. They promote schemes where the students have a strong 'buy-in' and they give the example of peer supporters choosing the colour of their badges and shirts (Moldrich and Carpentieri 2005). The Childline in Partnership with Schools (CHIPS) programme, one of the most experienced peer support training programmes in the UK, refers to its DfES evaluation report (Smith and Watson 2004). It states that 'even though schools can share good practice and learn from each other's successes and mistakes, peer support schemes, 'cannot be "parachuted in" from other schools.' They must be unique to each school. The Childline approach is to 'lay down the foundations for a peer support programme that will really work' (Childline 2002). The ideal is for training programmes to meet schools' current individual needs but in addition to sustain their peer support services so they can evolve as the schools' needs change.

Keeping up the momentum

Apart from internal strategies like launching and publicizing the services, joint projects with other schools, conferences and seminars all serve to keep motivation and enthusiasm high for staff and students. The Children Fund Project in Stafford in 2003/4 enabled two high schools and two of their feeder primary schools to work together to set up peer support using the same co-counselling model adapted for the different age groups. Peer mentoring was established in the high schools and befriending services were set up in the primary schools. The participants enjoyed getting together for a joint conference in 2004. In the previous joint conferences evaluations from students revealed initial nervousness about meeting peers from other schools but they experienced a growth in self-confidence and enthusiasm from the process of co-counselling with each other, sharing experiences and networking. Staff have also found it helpful discussing their work with others who co-ordinate peer support. Joint projects are especially useful as indicated by the headteacher of The Grove Primary School, Stafford:

'The benefit of working as four schools on the one project is the follow through from primary to high via Years 6 and 7 – this adds a pastoral dimension to the excellent transition arrangements now in place. What has helped our school in setting up and sustaining our peer support was the training for staff and pupils which was excellent and has been carried through. The early links with other schools also proved helpful' (Cartwright 2005).

In those schools where staff and students have attended national conferences on peer support, sustainability is high. This was the case with students from Walton Hall Community Special School (Case study 6 in Chapter 10) who gained much confidence from travelling to London for a National Peer Support Forum Conference. They assisted their trainer in leading a workshop and each led small support groups of eight young people and adults.

Supervision

All projects must have regular adult supervision otherwise peer supporters are at risk of feeling isolated and losing enthusiasm. Ideally supervisors monitor the service and provide guidance and support to the peer supporters on a weekly or fortnightly basis as well as being available for immediate concerns on a daily basis. They are also points of referral when peer supporters are taken beyond the limits of competency. The careful appointment of motivated and adaptable supervisors is needed and if necessary specialist support such as for sex or drugs education should be available. Students need to be constantly updated and to be clear about the boundaries of their competence and know when to refer users on to their supervisors. It is important for supervisors to have enough non-contact time for them to fulfil their role of supervising peer supporters during lunchtimes, morning or afternoon registration periods and/or other times such as PSHE lessons.

A supervision session during a morning 20 minute registration period/tutor time.

- The supervisor registers the peer supporters present for the administrative department while peer supporters are in pairs co-counselling on what has been going well and any difficulties with peer support work during the week. (5 minutes)
- A round of what has been going well and any difficulties with peer support work during the week. (5 minutes)
- Problem solving with other peer supporters and the supervisor making suggestions. (5 minutes)
- A round of plans for the next week with supervisor support if necessary. (5 minutes)

Supervision session

Child protection

Children and young people have a fundamental right to be protected from harm and to expect schools to provide a safe and secure environment. The basis of the law and child protection procedures is that the protection and welfare of the child must always be the first priority and is a shared community responsibility. Failure to provide an effective response can have serious consequences for the child. Teachers and other education staff are in a unique position to identify and help abused children, as are peer supporters and other students.

As such, they all need to be aware of the legal framework in which they work especially when providing a confidential service such as peer support. Before beginning to help or support another student a peer supporter must explain to the client the limits of confidentiality that exist. The following provides an example of a form of words that has proved useful, providing a 'mantra' for peer supporters.

The peer supporter's 'Mantra'

I can offer you a confidential service, which means I will keep what you tell me a secret. However, the law says that I cannot keep anything confidential if it means your health or life is at risk or the health or life of another person is at risk. If you tell me something like that or it involves some kind of physical or mental abuse I would have to tell one of the teachers or help you tell a teacher yourself.

The legal framework

During their training peer supporters and their supervisors need to be made aware of the key legislation that provides the legal context in which they work. The Children Act 2004, and its Welsh, Scottish and Northern Ireland equivalents, are the legislative authority for child welfare and protecting children from abuse. Sections 27 and 47 of the Children Act 1989 place duties on a number of agencies to assist social services departments enquiring into allegations of child abuse and acting on behalf of children and young people in need. It gives every child the right to protection from abuse and exploitation and the right to have enquiries made to safeguard their welfare. The other key act is The Protection of Children Act (PoCA) 1999 aiming to prevent paedophiles from working with children. The act applies to adults and is therefore not directly relevant to the work of peer supporters. However, school staffs need to bear in mind the risk of students being sexually abused by their peers and therefore the need for careful recruiting and vetting of volunteers.

Child protection in the context of peer support

The Children Acts 1989 and 2004 set out clear procedures for child protection in schools. These apply to all staff, though young people are not legally obliged to report to staff on material disclosed to them in confidence. For this reason it is critical to strongly emphasize the confidentiality arrangements and agreements for young people in peer support programmes. It is also critical that peer supporters are regularly supervised by at least one adult in a school (see Chapter 5). The procedures, which apply to adults in school according to the Children Act, have been adapted as guidelines for young people when they are training and working in the peer support role and for their supervisors (see opposite page).

Peer supporter explaining confidentiality

Child protection

If any member of staff or young peer supporter has any suspicion or is informed about abuse to a student, the matter must be reported immediately to the teacher in charge of child protection and responsible for liaising with other agencies and co-ordinating action within the school.

IF IN DOUBT REFER THE MATTER TO
THE TEACHER IN CHARGE OF CHILD PROTECTION

DO NOT:
1. Under ANY circumstances remove the child's clothing.
2. Contact the parents or guardians as your enquiries may be counterproductive. Leave this to other agencies such as social services and the police.
3. Give a promise to a child over keeping a secret without explaining the limits of confidentiality set by the Children Acts.

DO:
1. Note all the marks you have observed or which have been brought to your attention by the young person or anyone else. NO FURTHER EXAMINATION SHOULD BE CARRIED OUT.
2. Quote verbatim, if possible, all conversations with the young person (or anyone else, including parents, if they are aware).

DEFINITIONS OF ABUSE:
a) Physical Injury: Physical abuse may range from direct blows to chronic poisoning.
b) Physical Neglect: Lack of food, warmth and protection from danger that is necessary for all young people.
c) Emotional Injury: This can take the form of emotional abuse or cruelty and the only evidence may be abnormal behaviour seen in the young person.
d) Emotional Neglect: lack of love and attention that is essential for physical and emotional growth.
e) Sexual Abuse: This is the involvement of dependent, developmentally immature children and adolescents in sexual activities they do not truly comprehend, to which they are unable to give informed consent, which violate social taboos or family roles which are against the law.
f) Potential Abuse: Young people are entitled to protection from situations where they have not been abused but where social and medical assessments indicate a high degree of risk that they might be abused in the future.

Chapter 9

Assessment, monitoring, evaluation and accreditation

 Efficiency is doing things right; effectiveness is doing right things.

(Peter Drucker)

There are many ways of effectively assessing, monitoring and evaluating peer support that are accessible to young people of all abilities. They are all necessary processes for reviewing the outcomes and processes of a service from a variety of perspectives. They offer valuable knowledge and insight so that supervisors and peer supporters can improve and develop effectiveness in further development. Accreditation is not necessary for this and too much emphasis on it can be detrimental to the co-operative, non-competitive spirit of peer support. However, it can be useful as a means of giving credibility to and recognition of the skills and experience that peer supporters have acquired. This chapter firstly looks at assessment and then explores ways of monitoring and evaluating peer support projects. Finally it outlines possible routes of accreditation.

Assessment

This is a process where judgements are made by those involved about learning and development. The purpose of assessing the peer support process is to:

- Enable people to know what has been learned, secure commitment, and to promote self-esteem and emotional development.
- Develop students' skills of reflecting and to make learning real for them.
- Identify future learning needs.

- Enable recognition and celebration of progress in all areas especially meeting individual and group goals.
- Provide evidence of the impact of peer support for healthy schools work, quality assurance and formal accreditation if desired.

Assessment for this kind of active learning happens at different levels and stages in a cyclical process and includes a number of activities carried out by a range of people such as peer supporters, students using the service, teachers and learning mentors. It means assessing each part in the sequence of the active learning process shown below:

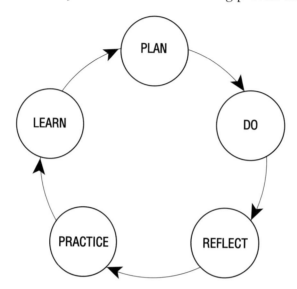

The Active Learning Cycle

Assessment activities usually include:

The recruitment process

This is the first point of assessment and involves identifying each applicant's needs and abilities. Students must be capable of paying enough attention as listeners to operate the service. If they are unable to do this sufficiently they would be unsuitable for counselling and mentoring training and could be offered other roles in a peer support service. A self-evaluation before the training may help students recognize whether they can peer support directly or whether they would prefer a different role in the service such as administration and publicity.

A baseline assessment

This assessment can be made of the learning needs of each applicant so that they can be matched to a suitable type of training and subsequent work as peer supporter. For example games on a training course would need to be adapted for varying physical abilities.

Formative assessment

This involves reflection on what has been learned and how to put this learning into action. The training course and the work as peer supporters can provide opportunities for this as part of the evaluation process (see later in this chapter). A quick-think exercise (see Chapter 4) at the beginning of each topic in the training can help identify what the students already know. This kind of assessment requires peer supporters analysing personal responses to the training course and subsequent peer support work. The trainer and the students can make self- and peer assessments of their abilities to be peer supporters during and after the training. They can judge progress made against the learning objectives of the course and project and use this to inform further work.

Questions for students to review their learning and plan for the future
(source: Blake 2005)

 ▶ What new information have I learned?
 ▶ What do I think and believe?
 ▶ Has listening to the views of others changed my views?
 ▶ Did I learn anything I did not expect to?
 ▶ How will my future behaviour be changed?
 ▶ What did I know already?
 ▶ How do I feel about what I found out?
 ▶ What do I need to learn next?
 ▶ Is there anyone else I need to talk to about this?

Summative assessment

This is done at the end of a period of time or a specific piece of work such as a training course. It involves the collection of information to demonstrate achievement and competence and to inform others. The monitoring and evaluation process described later in this chapter can provide this information as well as quizzes, questionnaires, role plays, problem-solving activities and peer supporters keeping their own personal records of self-development in diaries. These activities can provide evidence of progress judged in relation to peer supporters' action plans and/or a set of criteria such as the key stage indicators set out by the Qualifications and Curriculum Authority (QCA) (see Appendix 3). The results of the assessment can be used to report back to all stakeholders in the peer support process and be a basis for future sustaining and development of the programme.

Different approaches to assessment (based on Blake 2005)

Assessment for Learning

Private reflection	Regular entries in personal diary
Self-assessment	Directed consideration of diary entries, group-work activities
Peer assessment	Exchange of views between peers within the group
Peer assessment with other groups	Exchanging views with users of the peer support service, for example, Year 7 students
Structured informal assessment by adult	Ongoing observations, questioning, feedback to students
Structured formal assessment by adult	Quizzes, questionnaires, work samples, marked work for portfolios
External examination	Formal accreditation such as ASDAN, Edexcel and OCN

Assessment of Learning

Monitoring and evaluation

Monitoring involves keeping records of the activities and processes involved in a peer support programme. Evaluation is the process for judging the effectiveness of these particular activities, materials and approaches in meeting specific aims and objectives. Peer supporters' records of communications with their clients should be kept for their own personal use and care should be taken to protect anonymity. However, it is important to keep a record of how many and what type of students have used and benefited from a peer support service. For example peer mentors and/or mediators can keep records of the numbers of sessions when they have supported students. As part of this it is essential that identities are kept confidential and supervisors must ensure that they adhere to the Data Protection Act (see Children's Legal Centre 2001).

Monitoring the mentor/mediator service

Name of school:

▶ Please fill in the form below each time you support a student/two disputants who have come to you or the drop-in for help.

▶ Instead of putting their name give them a number (increasing sequentially). If they come again give them the same number every time they come.

▶ Under ethnicity write A (Asian) B (Black) W (White) or D/M (Dual/Mixed).

▶ Under type of problem write the main one. (Choose from: friends, home, parents, brothers, sisters, teachers, school work, in trouble at school, bullied, bully, illness, pet's illness, illness in family, pet's death, death in family). If none of these, write what it is.

▶ Under refer? put yes if the problem is too serious for you to deal with, and refer the problem to one of your teachers. Put no if you can deal with it yourself and keep it confidential.

Date	Number	Age	Ethnicity	Type of problem	Refer?

Evaluating the information gained from such a monitoring system helps in the reflection of the work and adds to judgement on what works well and not so well. It provides the chance for peer supporters, supervisors and senior school staff to revise practice and to refocus objectives in the light of the information. There are two main types of evaluation as follows:

1. *Impact evaluation*

    This is concerned with the long, medium and short term impact of peer support projects. When peer support is part of major national strategies such as Connexions, the Children's Fund and Healthy Schools they are evaluated in that way. Large initiatives in the interest of accountability tend to seek to measure changes in attitudes and behaviour over time as a result of the peer support programmes. This requires high levels of resources, time and expertise on the part of the evaluator who is usually independent rather than being part of a self-evaluation programme.

2. *Process evaluation*

This examines the delivery and practice of a training course and peer support programme, through reflection and feedback to enable immediate responses and future planning. Unlike impact evaluation, this tends to be based on self-evaluation and findings only utilized by the users of the project themselves. Questions could be:

- Was it possible to deliver the programme as planned? If not why not?
- How well did the content of the programme meet the needs of the target group?
- Did everyone participate?
- How far was the programme accessible to the target group?
- What worked well and less well? How could it be improved?

Process evaluation involves taking account of how peer supporters work together as a team and whether everyone participated and achieved at their own level. Consideration of how activities are organized and delivered can be helpful. Also evaluating the availability and appropriateness of resources is pertinent. The whole process promotes self-awareness, communication skills and a personal responsibility for learning.

Assessment and evaluation activities (source: Blake 2005)

- Quizzes involving verbal feedback.
- Role play demonstrating skills, knowledge and comprehension as well as exploring attitudes and values.
- Posters are useful when high literacy skills are not needed.
- Discussion and debate.
- Diaries for private reflection.
- Wordsearches.
- Group presentations, film making and assemblies to encourage team work.
- Group sculpture uses physical exercise to reflect feelings about peer support.
- Values continuum.
- Questionnaires and review sheets.

The ideal model of evaluation would be a combination of impact and process evaluation. This would involve both self-evaluation and an independent evaluator. Using the latter can be a participatory empowering process provided that the evaluation brief is designed with these principles in mind. However, schools very rarely commission an independent evaluator. Universities are obliged to charge full economic costing at a rate of 45 per cent for the use of premises, computers, libraries and administration so the cost would be prohibitive for most schools. The best way for a school to obtain an independent evaluation is to negotiate with a university to jointly apply to an external funding body so that both the school and the university benefit. For example, Keele University Psychology Department and the University of Surrey (Cowie et al. 2002) evaluated Walton High School. Where this level of evaluation is adhered to it is more likely that a school will sustain its project over time. The reasons for this are twofold: it means the school is truly committed; and the level and quality of the evaluation feedback is such that it boosts the peer support programme.

The simplest way for a school to monitor, assess and evaluate its peer support process is to do it 'in house'. For this a system needs to be designed where data is collected and collated systematically. When preparing the assessment and evaluation activities it is also important to ensure that they focus on the key messages the students are to learn and are accessible to students of all abilities. After collating and analysing the data collected in this way an evaluation report can be written and distributed to all stakeholders in the peer support project. See Appendix 4 for examples of questionnaires and their analysis; and review sheets and presentation of the collated data. The box below shows the key elements in an evaluation report.

The elements most commonly found in evaluation reports

▶ Description of the project
▶ Description of the methodology
▶ Presentation of the collated data
▶ Analysis of the data
▶ Recommendations.

Accreditation

Some schools accredit peer support courses so their student workers have recognized certification based on the school's own assessment criteria. They are usually carried out in relation to national targets to see if a certain standard has been reached. Students usually aged 14 upwards can train on an accredited course from the Open College Network (OCN) to levels NVQ 1 and 2 or with other voluntary agencies. The Award Scheme Development Accreditation Network (ASDAN) offers structured formal assessment opportunities for Key Stages 3 and 4 contributing to a national accreditation. Other examples of routes to accreditation are Edexcel and the Life Routes Programme at the National Children's Bureau. More details of these accreditation schemes and their websites are in Appendix 3.

There are advantages and disadvantages with accreditation. For many students and their adult supervisors the processes involved in the training and subsequent peer support service have their own value and accreditation detracts from this if it takes up too much time and involves too much ticking of boxes. Training programmes can even be distorted in order to fit the criteria demanded by the accreditation schemes. However, it can be argued that young people who have devoted much time and energy in their training and running of their services deserve to have their work accredited. It can also give credibility to and recognition of the skills and experience they have acquired especially when they are pursuing their future careers.

Added Power and Understanding in Sex Education (APAUSE), a multi-agency programme of sex education, designed two accreditation routes for their peer educators (see www.departments.ex.ac.uk/childhealth/publications/ and Case study 8 in Chapter 10). The first was to establish mechanisms whereby Year 12 and Year 13 peer educators can receive academic credit through existing links to mainstream qualifications for their training and subsequent work carried out. This may be directly relevant to modules in some curriculum subjects and vocational courses and to many AS levels as well as the new Key Skills curriculum undertaken by all students in post-16 education.

In addition a new performance-based qualification for peer educators was developed based on professional assessment of the peer educators in authentic practice in the classroom. This was developed with a draft syllabus for the qualification in Peer Education (Sex and Relationships). APAUSE were in negotiation with QCA for it to be accredited as a national qualification but this process at the time of writing has yet to be completed (Morgan et al. 2004).

Chapter 10

They do it this way: examples of good practice in the long term

 There must be a beginning of any great matter, but the continuing unto the end until it be thoroughly finished yields the full glory.

(Sir Francis Drake)

Since the early days of peer support in the UK, many schools have sustained their service over many years as part of an ongoing process of promoting young people's full participation in schools and society. The 'full glory' of that process finishing can only be imagined but peer support programmes are one of the many initiatives that provide glimpses of a society where young people have an equal voice with that of adults. The strength of peer support schemes lies in the commitment of their staff and students, the funds and resources available, the quality of training and the adaptability of the schemes to meet their own specific needs. Also important is the careful selection of students; maintaining the momentum; networking and sharing experiences; and regular monitoring and evaluation. In order for all this to happen in the long term the commitment and direct involvement from senior management is needed. This chapter is devoted to examples of schools illustrating these key strengths over many years. The first example is the school that pioneered peer support in the 1980s. The longevity of the programme can be attributed to the constant support from senior management and to highly committed, self-motivated and fully trained co-ordinators.

Case Study 1

Walton High School, Staffordshire: an example of long term commitment to peer counselling as an anti-bullying strategy (Cartwright 2003)

Walton High School has been committed to peer support since 1985. It was the first school in the UK to initiate an organized system. It is a large comprehensive school in a county town with a mostly middle class and predominantly white intake of about 1,200 students aged 11–18. It was also one of the earliest schools in the UK to initiate an anti-bullying policy with peer support as a major strategy. A 'positive' atmosphere has been conducive to its anti-bullying policy which began in 1990. Various indicators suggest that there has been a reduction in bullying and a raising of security with the severity and frequency of physical and property bullying falling to relatively low levels. Both staff and student interviewed for the Keele University Anti-Bullying Project showed a high awareness of anti-bullying work and support for the policy (Glover and Cartwright 1998). There is a history of strong commitment from senior management, which has enabled staff to have enough time to do the work of supervising and training the students. The peer support service has evolved and changed over the years but the basic system is peer supporters as buddies having weekly contact with Year 7 students coupled with a drop-in and mediation service for the whole school. Over the 20 years the service has included:

- Volunteer students and staff being taught on an annual basis a modified co-counselling skills course originally based on the Re-evaluation Co-counselling (RC) model.

- Four trained staff who supervise and train the students so that if any staff leave the system can still be maintained.

- A room dedicated as a drop-in where for two lunchtimes a week two peer listeners are ready to give one-to-one listening and/or mediation support.

- A co-counselling club where peer supporters have led and taught others how to co-counsel.

After the original co-ordinator left the school in 2000 the management fully supported her replacements, two staff who had both completed a 40 hour RC course. They have continued and developed the service with peer supporters presenting at national conferences.

Case Study 2

Longton High School, Stoke-on-Trent: four years of predominantly white led peer support followed by five years of white and Asian peer mentors (Cartwright 2005)

The school described by peer supporters as 'a large comprehensive on top of a hill' on a mostly council housing estate on the edge of Stoke-on-Trent, took part alongside 24 other Midlands school in the Keele University Anti-bullying Project which showed that bullying was a serious issue in their school as elsewhere (Cartwright 1996). In response the school decided to set up peer support in 1997 as an anti-bullying strategy.

Given the school has a sizeable Muslim population and an active British National Front in the local community, there is a history of racial conflict which increased dramatically after 9/11. Netta Cartwright, had already been training students as peer supporters since 1997 but the few Asian students who participated often dropped out after the first day. Feeling uncomfortable as a minority they requested an Asian only class. A service for Year 7 and 8 Asian students was established in 2001 with a follow-up workshop for white and Asian buddies who decided on a joint drop-in for white and Asian students. There is now a joint white and Asian peer mentoring service with mixed buddy teams allotted to each Year 7 tutor group; and support for Year 6 on induction days and their first day at school. Small teams of Asian and white buddies lead anti-bullying lessons. They also represented the school at meetings of the Peer Support Forum and wrote a report as follows:

'The kinds of problems students face are racial and bullying problems such as harassment, name calling, violence and singling out occurring both in between lessons on the school's corridors, and during break and dinner. The school has had a few major racial disputes but mainly faced with minor disputes between students, which with the skills we have been taught through our training, we are confident to deal with.'

Over the years various types of mentoring services have been provided as follows:

- A mentor scheme for Asian students in Years 7 and 8 providing each student with a trained Asian student as mentor.
- Group sessions arranged for mentors and mentees once every half-term in PSHE lessons and informal contact the rest of the time.
- A drop-in for students from all years to have one-to-one counselling.
- A team of two or three Asian and white buddies going into each Year 7 tutor group regularly about once a week or every two weeks.
- Small teams of Asian and white buddies leading anti-bullying PSHE lessons.
- Asian and white buddies supporting Year 6 on induction days and when they start as Year 7s for the first time.

Asian mentor and mentee

Case Study 3

Hagley Park Sports College, Rugeley, Staffordshire: eight years of peer mentoring with smooth transition in supervision changeover

This school, which serves a working class area of a small town, set up a peer support 'buddy' system in 1998. The teacher who led it completed a 40-hour RC counselling course with Netta Cartwright, helped train the first two cohorts of buddies and remained until 2005 as trainer and supervisor. Peer supporters operated a drop-in room five days a week and a playground patrol system looking for isolated children and any other problems. When the supervisor left the school in 2005 and another teacher took over her role as buddy tutor. This new supervisor and 20 Year 11 buddies were trained for one day by Peer Support Works using a basic version of the co-counselling model to cover: negotiation, mediation, peer support counselling, and anti-bullying awareness and strategies. The supervisor trained another 25 Year 10 students and in-school refresher training is ongoing despite difficulties getting permission for buddies to have time out of lessons for training. This as well as the peer support service is run regularly by the Buddy Team Staff, which at the time of writing consists of the buddy tutor, Sue Stoker, supported by two behaviour managers, Claire Aldridge and Sam Brownless.

Sue Stoker described the service to the author as providing:

'Year 7 and Year 8 students with older "buddies" who they feel able to chat to and confide in about anything – from worries about school or home, advice on homework or clubs to bullying of themselves or their peers. Each Year 7/8 tutor group has been allocated its own two buddies who visit their class once or more a week, usually during registration. The students become familiar with their buddies and learn to trust them. The buddies lead activities such as class and group games to teach the younger pupils assertiveness skills, so building up their confidence and self-esteem.'

The Buddy Drop-In is a dedicated room staffed by two buddies on a rota each lunchtime. Sue Stoker explained that:

'They are available for students to go in and chat to, to share any concerns with and to receive advice and support from buddies. The buddies are trained to ask neutral questions and to use supportive listening skills. All worries or incidents are treated seriously. Any bullying which has been reported to a buddy is dealt with promptly. This reassures the pupils concerned, helps them to feel happier and stops further bullying.'

All issues are recorded in the Confidential Buddy Folder and checked by the supervisor at the end of each lunchtime. They are sorted out by the buddies confidentially, or, if necessary, referred on to the Buddy Team Staff using a referral form designed by one of the buddies as part of a competition (see Appendix 4). All incidents are dealt with the same day and tutors are informed. The buddies regularly monitor any students who have been to see them.

The local community officer acquired funds to purchase buddy logo jackets as well as buddy badges to help make them more easily recognizable around the school premises. In response to requests from students, a very popular buddy activity club has been opened two lunchtimes a week with a pool table, board games and role play, all designed to increase the confidence of students and encourage co-operation and the making of new friends. One activity involved designing an anti-bullying booklet for a competition.

Sue Stoker commented on the impact of the activity club on the students and also the impact of the buddy scheme on the local community:

'There have been bullies and victims of bullying working alongside and in harmony with the buddies and each other. It has been fantastic and is very popular. Other schools have heard about us and several parents have remarked on how impressed they are with the Buddy System which we have in place. We even had a visit from a Head and Deputy Head of a nearby school who also want to start a Buddy Scheme in their school which is encouraging.'

Case Study 4

The Tamworth Peer Support for Inclusion Project: an example of individual programmes for individual schools (Cartwright 2005)

This two-year project began in 2004 and involves five high schools, a special school and a pupil referral unit (PRU) in Tamworth. As part of the project each school has set up peer mentoring for their Year 7 students and peer support for students moving between the PRU, the special school and the high schools. After leading a conference for student and staff representatives for all schools to launch the project, Netta Cartwright of Peer Support Works taught the staff a three-day co-counselling course. This was followed by three-day courses for students in each school led by their trained staff and Netta Cartwright. In addition selected students from each school were taught a three-day course focusing on supporting students moving between schools and students in danger of being excluded. Nearly all the high schools have begun or are moving towards mentoring support for students who have been suspended.

Case Study 5

Monitoring a befriending service at Castlechurch Primary School, Stafford (Cartwright 2005)

After the staff and first cohort of Year 6 students in 2003 were trained by Netta Cartwright they organized a befriending service which formalized their natural inclination to offer support and friendship to others of a similar age in everyday interactions (Cowie and Wallace 2000). Ten girls and eight boys are on a rota leading a lunchtime drop-in for rainy days and use the playground informally to befriend and support other pupils. They build up relationships with and actively seek out students who seem alone. They intervene in aggressive situations using mediation to calm students and encourage them to listen to each other so that they can reach agreed solutions. They record confidential notes on events and have access to three trained staff members to discuss concerns confidentially. These staff trained the second cohort. As well as helping 46 individual children the buddies have been mentors to four children who are having specific behaviour problems with two buddies per child.

An evaluation conducted by the school found that of the 42 girls and four boys aged 8 to 11 supported from October 2004 to January 2005, several were helped more than once and a few up to six times. The most common problems were friendship (51 occasions) and fallings out (8). Others were: game disputes, no friends, name calling, past events, being rough, being bullied, younger children, groups, family problems and rumours. In their evaluations the buddies said what they gained most from this was more friends, having fun and learning new things. They thought the children gained most from: the confidentiality; being helped to solve problems; and getting more friends. What they found difficult about being a buddy was not knowing what to say, not giving advice and keeping secrets. Another drawback was not playing with or talking to friends at lunchtimes while on duty. They enjoyed the training days for learning different skills, activities and games but they disliked missing good lessons. Their ideas for future improvements to their service were to improve the drop-in centre and to develop their skills.

Case Study 6

Formal one-to-one, peer counselling leading to students as active stakeholders at Walton Hall Community Special School, Staffordshire (Cartwright 2005)

Walton Hall Community Special School is an all age, including post-16, special school with 130 students who all have a statement of special needs and have learning difficulties. In addition many have associated emotional, physical, behavioural, speech, hearing and autism problems. After Netta Cartwright trained two of the staff in 2002 on a 40-hour RC course they assisted her in training the first two groups of eight post-16 students who were partly volunteers and partly selected for a 15-hour course. Students and staff continue to use co-counselling to support each other one-to-one. Some students have been counselling other students who were not on the course one-to-one and use the process to support younger residents at the school. They recently launched an active anti-bullying campaign with a dramatic play and continue to meet for an hour and a half fortnightly for an ongoing training programme of co-counselling. The headteacher sums it up.

'Our Buddy Group work has not only helped others but empowered the BG students – they are more proactive, confident and able to provide an excellent support system for our residential youngsters.'

He gives an example of Andrew aged 17 who started training this year:

'We have seen his confidence grow, he listens more to others, is proactive in helping other students now and will encourage free-flow feelings. He is able to follow through this training within the main school with other pupils.'

Much of the 'Buddy Group' work has helped develop their Schools Council, which has encouraged student participation, decision making and empowerment:

'Youngsters are real stakeholders – we have a pupil interview panel for staff appointments as standard now, have taken part in Active Youth Work in the County, have even been used to help the DfES launch its Special Educational Needs strategy. Recently they have been involved in developing the Oasis Centre – a sanctuary where pupils can chill out, talk and socialize. The development has made our lunchtimes much better. Would we have even considered this three years ago? Without the Buddy Group work and its impact on pupils, our youngsters would not have been as effective as stakeholders in the school community, would not have supported or been as tolerant of individuals. It has helped us to achieve real inclusion. We have IQM (Inclusion Quality Mark) status. Buddy Group is an active ingredient of a successful inclusive school.'

Case Study 7

Email peer support at Wolstanton High School, Newcastle under Lyme, Staffordshire
(Cartwright 2005)

This service evolved from the face to face listening outlined in Case Study 7 on page 22. Peer counsellors realized that some students were not confident enough to go to the drop-in service so an email address and posting box was set up. In 2001 a website was designed by one of the peer supporters with a page that could be forwarded as an email to their 'agony aunts and uncles'. These students regularly check the email and post box in the school foyer. They replied either via email or usually by coaxing the sender to come to the lunchtime drop-in. An example of a letter is:

'Dear BULLYinc,
All my friends have stopped speaking to me. They're not calling me names or anything –
they're just ignoring me. I think this is a form of bullying so I wrote for help – what
should I do?'

A peer supporter replied:

'You did the right thing by asking for help and I'm glad you realized that this can be a
form of bullying. Have you tried talking to your friends to find out why they aren't talking
to you? If you haven't then maybe you could try this. If they are still ignoring you
remember there are over 1,000 other pupils in the school that you can make friends with.
There are always people available to talk to and there is a BULLYinc club being set up for
people in similar situations as you, to meet with new people and to communicate their
problems to other pupils. I hope this has been helpful to you and given you the courage to
find new friends.'

Over six years the peer work at this school developed from peer research to include face to face counselling, mentoring and email support. They participated in a video for the Peer Support Forum and shared experiences at a local conference for two schools in the Stoke-on-Trent area and participant in two Youth Voice Peer Power events run by the Trust for Study of Adolescence. All this was student led with the support of an encouraging co-ordinator and senior management.

Case Study 8

APAUSE (Added Power and Understanding in Sex Education): Peer education programme working towards accreditation for peer educators

APAUSE began in 1990 as a research project in two Exeter schools and became a programme running in 30 schools across Devon and Torbay, supported by Devon Curriculum Services (DCA) and funded by the local primary care trusts. Developed from original research, APAUSE is a theory-based, behaviourally effective sex and relationships education programme, supporting effective sex and relationships education within the PSHE and citizenship framework. As a collaboration between Education and Health working with, and for, young people the programme is now firmly established as a service provision in 13 different Health/Education areas across England and Wales. Currently more than 16,000 young people per year group in approximately 150 schools are involved and new areas are regularly adopting this innovative peer led approach. The programme includes offering curriculum support to participating schools in a Year 7/8 programme developing work from National Curriculum, Key Stage 3, Science.

The long term goal is to promote the positive aspects of relationships, both emotional and physical in a context of public health benefit. More specifically, the objectives of the project are to:

- increase tolerance, respect and mutual understanding;
- enhance knowledge of risks and counteracting myths;
- improve effective contraceptive use by teenagers who are already sexually active;
- provide effective skills to those who wish to resist unwelcome pressure.

The WISE Project, Negotiations for Adolescent Sexual Health, is an example of one of their peer led projects. It addresses the issues of: the kinds of negotiations young people need to have for enjoying good sexual and relational health; and how these negotiation skills can be learned in the classroom situation. David Evans, of IMÙLÈ Theatre, worked with groups of young people to develop three scripted performance workshops delivered by Year 11 GCSE drama students to Year 10 PSHE students. These were entitled: 'Starting a relationship', 'Taking things a bit further' and 'Safer sex and accessing health care services'. The workshops acknowledged that many negotiations of an intimate nature take place with little or no verbal dialogue. These were explored using floor puppets and solutions were found through interactive theatre techniques. The third session included a visiting health professional who facilitated the class in the rehearsal of necessary negotiations in accessing health care provision.

The project was successfully piloted in six schools with an impact evaluation showing very positive results. An adaptation of the WISE Project has also been piloted as part of the Year 10 English Syllabus (AQA Combined English Language and Literature). It was also sponsored by The Department of Health to be replicated in the large conurbation of Manchester, Salford and Trafford where teenage pregnancy rates are high and there are significant levels of social exclusion. The development began in six pilot schools in September 2001 and now involves 13 schools across the conurbation. The Project is available to any school irrespective of their involvement with the main APAUSE programme and comes with a comprehensive training programme for teachers including a manual with video support materials in CD-ROM, DVD or VHS formats.

Another project is RAP (Respect and Protect) for young people not in mainstream secondary education (www.programmes.ex.ac.uk/apause/rtresearch.htm). The peer educators have themselves experienced seriously disrupted education and life in institutions outside mainstream education. Using drama-based techniques they explore key themes in sexual and relational health issues that threaten to keep 'at risk' young people in a state of permanent social exclusion. As the material is developed, so are the social and performance skills of the peer educators. Through a series of pilots in such institutions as Pupil Referral Units, School Inclusion Units and Young Mums Units the team has successfully compiled a series of six sessions run by peer educators each lasting approximately 90 minutes. The long term aim of this project is to make materials and processes widely available so that appropriately trained workers in the field can establish their own peer led programme both drawing from and contributing to the growing body of good practice established by RAP.

Two accreditation routes were designed by APAUSE for their peer supporters. The first was to establish mechanisms whereby Year 12 and Year 13 peer educators can receive academic credit through existing links to mainstream qualifications for their training and subsequent work carried out (see Chapter 9). The second was a performance-based qualification for peer educators based on professional assessment of the peer educators in authentic practice in the classroom. At the time of writing APAUSE are in negotiation with the Qualifications and Curriculum Authority for formal submission and approvals to have it accredited as a national qualification (Morgan 2004).

This final chapter has provided examples of a number of schools in which peer support projects have been developed over several years to become part of the fabric of everyday school life. The energy and commitment of the young people leading and using the peer support services and their adult allies has been a significant factor in this achievement. Peer support in the long term has the potential to improve life in schools but also has an impact on life beyond school and in the wider community. Having evaluated most of the schools referred to in this book, a key finding is the long term positive impact peer support can have on individual children: of those students, who have used a peer support service (whether as mentors or as clients), many go on to become peer supporters themselves. For example, on leaving school, some return as volunteers to help with training peer supporters, such as at Walton High School. Many have gone on to use their peer support skills in their careers and family life. Others have become teachers themselves and set up peer support in their schools, such as the buddy supervisor at Hagley Park Sports College who was a peer supporter at Walton High School.

Over the past 20 years peer support in its many forms has become part of everyday life in increasing numbers of schools. It has been a vital part of a national and worldwide movement towards systemic change to normalize school student participation. As such peer support has a critical role to play in current UK government initiatives promoting young people's citizenship and participation (See Appendix 2). This book has given an overview of the role of peer support today alongside the historical context and theories underpinning peer support programmes and their benefits. The wide variety and range of peer support projects has been explored and exemplary case studies and training courses provided for the most popular types of programmes. The focus of this book has been on the value of peer support as a long term initiative and how best to sustain the programmes over many years.

As required by the Education Act 2002, schools are now concerned with embedding participation into everyday practice and ensuring that the skills and learning are consolidated and rewarded. This involves a fundamental and continuing shift in the beliefs, values, approaches and changes in school systems and structures. In spring 2005 the National Children's Bureau surveyed advisers, consultants, inspectors and others involved in supporting school based PSHE, including peer support. Most respondents thought that participation needed to be much better developed in all areas of school life but felt that there was a keenness and growing acceptance of its value in schools despite often being detached from curriculum learning (NCB 2006). Ultimately peer support, as part of the wider participation agenda, is pivotal to changing the culture of schools by providing a mechanism for enabling the voices and actions of students to contribute to decision making in meaningful and sustained ways.

References

Baginsky, M. (2001), 'Peer support: what schools expect and what schemes can deliver', Paper presented at British Educational Research Association Conference, September 2001

Barrett, W. and Randall, L. (2001), *Circle of Friends Resource Pack*, Falkirk Council Psychological Service

Blake, S. (2005), *Assessment and Evaluation in Personal, Social and Health Education (PSHE)*, London: National Children's Bureau

Bodine, R., Crawford, D. and Schrumpf, F. (1994), *Creating the Peaceable School: A Comprehensive Program for Teaching Conflict Resolution*, Champaign, I: Research Press

Boehm, K., Chessare, J., Valko, T. and Sager, M. (1991), 'Teen Line', *Adolescence*, 26 (103), 643–648

Britton, F. (2000), *Active Citizenship: a teaching toolkit*, CSV Education for Citizenship, London: Hodder and Stoughton

Brooks, L. (2006), 'We can have sex so why can't we vote?', *The Guardian*, 28.02.06

Burley, S., Gutkin, T. and Naumann, W. (1994), 'Assessing the efficacy of an academic hearing peer tutor for a profoundly deaf student', *American Annals of the Deaf*, 139 (4), 415–419

California Association of Peer Programs (CAPP) (1998), 'Comprehensive Evaluation of Peer Programs', The California Wellness Foundation

Carr, R. (1988), 'The city-wide peer counselling program', *Children and Youth Services Review*, 10: 217–232

Carr, R. (1994), 'Peer Helping in Canada', *Peer Counselling Journal*, 11(1), 6–9

Cartwright, N.(1996), 'Combatting Bullying in School: the Role of Peer Helpers' in Cowie, H. and Sharp, S. (ed) (1996), *Peer Counselling in Schools: a time to listen*, London: David Fulton

Cartwright, N. (2003), 'Peer Support at Walton High School in Staffordshire', *The Emotional Literacy Handbook: Promoting whole-school strategies*, pg 64 Antidote, London: David Fulton Publishers

Cartwright, N. (2005), 'Setting up and sustaining peer support systems in a range of schools over 20 years', *Pastoral Care in Education*, 23, No.2, June

Childline, (2002), *Setting up a peer support scheme*, London: Childline

Children and Young People Unit, (2002), *Learning to Listen: Core Principles for the Involvement of Children and Young People*, London: CYPU, www.cypu.gov.uk

Children's Legal Centre (2001), *Offering Children Confidentiality and the Law*, Colchester: Children's Legal Centre

Christopher, J.S., Hansen, D.J. and MacMillan, V.M. (1991), 'Effectiveness of a peer-helper intervention to increase children's social interactions: Generalization, maintenance, and social validity', *Behavior Modification*, 15 (1), 22–50

Clements, I. and Buczkiewicz, M. (1993), *Approaches to Peer-led Health Education: a guide for youth workers*, London: Health Education Authority

Cowie, H. and Hutson, N. (2005), 'Peer Support: A Strategy to Help Bystanders Challenge School Bullying', *Pastoral Care in Education*, 23, No.2, June

Cowie, H., Naylor, P., Talamelli, L., Chauhan, P. and Smith P.K. (2002), 'Knowledge, use of and attitudes towards peer support: a two-year follow-up of the Prince's Trust survey', *Journal of Adolescence*, 25 (5), 453–467

Cowie, H. and Olafsson, R. (2000), 'The Role of Peer Support in Helping the Victims of Bullying in Schools with a High Level of Aggression', *School Psychology International*, 21(1), 79–95

Cowie, H. and Sharp, S. (eds) (1996), *Peer Counselling in Schools: A Time to Listen*, London: David Fulton

Cowie, H., Smith, P.K., Boulton, M. and Laver, R. (1994), *Co-operation in the multi-ethnic Classroom*, London: David Fulton

Cowie, H. and Wallace, P. (2000), Peers Support in Action: from bystanding to standing by, London: Sage Publications

Creese, A. Norwich, B. and Daniels, H. (2000), Evaluating Teacher Support Teams in Secondary Schools: supporting teachers for SEN and other needs, *Research Papers in Education*, 15 (3), 307–324

Daniels, H. (ed.) (1996), 'Psychology in a Social World', *Introduction to Vygotsky*, London: Routledge

Demetriades, A. (1996), 'Children of the Storm: peer partnership', in Cowie. H. and Sharp. S. (eds) *Peer Counselling in Schools: a Time to Listen*. London: David Fulton, pp 64–72

Department for Education and Employment /Qualification and Curriculum Authority (1999), *The National Curriculum: Handbook for secondary teachers in England: Key Stages* 3 and 4, London: DfEE and QCA

Department for Education and Skills (2000), *Connexions – The Best Start in Life for Every Young Person*, London: DfES

Department of Education and Skills (2002), *Don't Suffer in Silence*, London: DfES

Department for Education and Skills (2003), *Every Child Matters*, London: DfES

Department for Education and Skills (2004a), *The Children Act*, London: DfES

Department of Education and Skills (2004b), *Working Together: Giving children and young people a say*, London: DfES

Department for Education and Skills (2005a), *Extended Schools: Access to opportunities and services for all – a prospectus*, London: DfES

Department for Education and Skills (2005b), *Higher Standards, Better Schools for All – More Choice for Parents and Pupils*, London: DfES

Department for Education and Skills (2005c), *Youth Matters*, London: DfES

Department for Education and Skills (2006a), *Youth Matters: Next Steps*, London: DfES

Department for Education and Skills (2006b), *Education and Inspections Bill*, London: DfES

Department for Education and Skills and Department of Health (2005), *National Healthy School Status: A guide for schools*, London: Department of Health

Department of Health and The Home Office (2003), *Report on the Victoria Climbié Inquiry by Lord Laming*, London: The Stationery Office

Elton, R.E. (1989), *Discipline in Schools: The report of the committee chaired by Lord Elton*, Norwich: HMSO/DES

Evans, R., Pinnock, K., Beirens, H. and Edwards, A. (2006), *Developing Preventative Practices: The Experiences of Children, Young People and their Families in the Children's Fund*, National Evaluation of the Children's Fund, University of Birmingham

Foot, H., Morgan, M. and Shute, R. (eds) (1990), *Children Helping Children*, Chichester: Wiley

Franca, V. et al. (1990), 'Peer tutoring among behaviourally disordered students: academic and social benefits to tutor and tutee', *Education and Treatment of Children* 17, 267–276

Glover, D. and Cartwright, N. (1998), *Towards Bully-free Schools*, Buckingham: Open University Press

Hahn, J. and LeCapitaine, J.E. (1990), 'The impact of peer counseling upon the emotional development, ego development, and self-concepts of peer counselors', *College Student Journal*, 24 (4), 410–420

Harnett, R. (2003), *Peer advocacy for children and young people*, Highlight number 202, National Children's Bureau

Hartley-Brewer, E. (2002), Stepping Forward: Working together through peer support. London: National Children's Bureau Enterprises Ltd.

Hill, M. (2006), *Parenting and children's resilience in disadvantaged communities*, National Children's Bureau on behalf of the Joseph Rowntree Foundation

Jackins, H. (1965), *Basic Postulates of Re-evaluation Counselling*. Seattle: Rational Island Publishing

James, J., Charlton, T., Leo, E. and Indoe, D. (1991), 'Using peer counsellors to improve secondary pupils' spelling and reading performance', *Maladjustment and Therapeutic Education*, 9 (1), 33–40

Kauffman, K. and New, C. (2004), *Co-Counselling: The Theory and Practice of Re-evaluation Counselling*, Hove and New York: Brunner-Routledge

King, P. and Occleston, S. (1998), 'Shared Learning in Action: children can make a difference', *Health Education*, 3, 100–106

Kirby, P., Lanyon, C., Cronin, K. and Sinclair, R. (2003), *Building a Culture of Participation: Involving children and young people in policy, service planning, delivery and evaluation (Handbook and Research Report)*, National Children's Bureau and PK Research Consultancy, London: DfES

Konet, R., (1991) 'Peer helpers in the middle school', *Middle School Journal*, September 13–16

Lane, P., McWhirter,J., and Jeffries, J. (1992), 'A peer mediation model: conflict resolution for elementary and middle school children', *Elementary School Guidance and Counseling*, 27 (1), 15–23

Le Surf, P. and Lynch, G. (1999), 'Exploring young people's perceptions relevant to counselling: a qualitative study' in Lynch, G. (ed), *Clinical Counselling in Pastoral Settings* London: Routledge

Lewis, M.W. and Lewis, A.C. (1996), 'Peer helping programs: Helper role, supervisor training, and suicidal behavior', *Journal of Counseling & Development*, 74 (3), 307–313

Lloyd, K. (2000), *OCN Introduction to Community Mediation Skills*, Wolverhampton Mediation Service

Lowenstein, L. (1989), 'The peer group promoting socialised behaviour: how can the peer group be mobilised to counteract and remedy negative behaviour?', *Education Today*, 39 (2), 27–34

McGee, G.G., Almeida, M.C., Sulzer-Azaroff, B. and Feldman, R.S. (1992), 'Promoting reciprocal interactions via peer incidental teaching', *Journal of Applied Behavior Analysis*, 25 (1), 117–126

McGowan, M. (2002), *Young People and Peer Support: How to set up a peer support programme*, Trust for the Study of Adolescence.

Mellanby, A.R., Rees, J.B., Tripp, J.H. (2000), 'Peer-led and adult-led school health education: a critical review of available comparative research', *Health Education Research*, 15 (5), 533–545

Moldrich, C. and Carpentieri J.D., (2005), *Every school should have one: How peer support schemes make schools better*, London: Childline

Morgan, D. (2004), *Report on Peer Accreditation Project to Teenage Pregnancy Unit* Exeter: APAUSE

Morgan, D.L., Robbins, J. and Tripp, J. (2004), 'Celebrating the Achievements of Sex and Relationship Peer Educators: The Development of an Assessment Process', *Sex Education*, 4 (2), 176–183

National Children's Bureau (2005), *Healthy Care Training Manual: A health promotion training programme for foster carers and residential social workers*, London: National Children's Bureau.

National Children's Bureau (2006a), *Personal, Social and Health Education: A snapshot survey of current issues and trends*, London: National Children's Bureau

National Children's Bureau (2006b), *A whole-school approach to Personal, Social and Health Education and Citizenship*, London: National Children's Bureau

National Healthy School Standard and Healthy Care (2004), *Promoting Children and Young People's Participation through the NHSS*, London: Health Development Agency

Naylor, P. (1997), *Peer Support Systems as a Challenge to Bullying in Schools: Some recent research findings on their effectiveness*, School of Psychology and Counselling, Roehampton Institute

Naylor, P. and Cowie, H. (1999), 'The effectiveness of peer support systems in challenging school bullying: the perspectives and experiences of teachers and pupils', *Journal of Adolescence* 22, 467–479

Newton, C., Taylor, G., and Wilson, D., (1996), 'Circle of Friends – An Inclusive Approach to Meeting Emotional and Behavioural Needs', *Educational Psychology in Practice*, 11, 4, 41–48

Newton, C. and Wilson, D. (1999), *Circles of Friends*, Dunstable: Folens

Newton, C. and Wilson, D. (2003), *Creating Circles of Friends: A Peer Support and Inclusion Workbook*, Nottingham: Inclusive Solutions

Perske, R. (1988), *Circle of Friends*, London: Abingdon Press

Qualification and Curriculum Authority (1999), *The Secretary of State's Proposals for the Review of the National Curriculum in England*, London: QCA

Quarmby, D. (1993), 'Peer counselling with bereaved adolescents', *British Journal of Guidance and Counselling*, 21 (2), 196–211

Rogers, C. (1957), 'The necessary and sufficient conditions of therapeutic personality change', *Journal of Consulting Psychology*, 21, 95–103

Rogers, K., Scherer-Thompson, J. and Laws, S. (1999), *Peer Support Programme: Report on the Findings from Stage 1 of the Evaluation.* London: The Mental Health Foundation

Rowan, J. (1976), *Ordinary Ecstasy: Human Psychology in Action*, London: Routledge

Scheff, T. (1972), 'Re-evaluation counselling: Social Implication' *Journal of Humanistic Psychology*, 12 (1)

Scherer-Thompson, J. (2002), *Peer Support Manual: A guide to setting up a peer listening project in education settings*, London: Mental Health Foundation

Sharp, S. and Cowie, H. (1998), *Counselling and supporting children in distress*, London: Sage

Sharp, S., Sellors, A. and Cowie, H. (1994), 'Time to listen: setting up a peer counselling service to help tackle the problem of bullying in schools', *Pastoral Care in Education*, 12 (2), 3–6

Shiner, M. (2000), *Doing it for themselves: an evaluation of approaches to drugs prevention*, Drugs Prevention Advisory Service (DPAS), London: Home Office

Shotton, G. (1998), 'A Circle of Friends approach for socially neglected children', *Educational Psychology in Practice*, 14 (1), 22–25

Silver, E.J., Coupey, S.M., Bauman, L.J. and Doctors, S.R. (1992), 'Effects of a peer counseling training intervention on psychological functioning of adolescents', *Journal of Adolescent Research*, 7 (1), 110–128

Simmons, D.C., Fuchs, L.S., Fuchs, D., Mathes, P. and Hodge, J.P. (1995), 'Effects of explicit teaching and peer tutoring on the reading achievement of learning-disabled and low-performing students in regular classrooms'. *Elementary School Journal*, 95, 387–408

Smith, P.K. and Sharp, S. (eds) (1994), *School Bullying: Insights and Perspectives*, London: Routledge

Smith, P. and Watson, D. (2004), *An Evaluation of the Childline in Partnership with Schools (CHIPS) Programme*, Department for Education and Skills research report RR570

Somers, B. (1972), 'Re-evaluation Therapy: Theoretical Framework', *Journal of Humanistic Psychology* (1), Spring Issue

Sprinthall, N., Hall, J. and Gerber, E.(1992), 'Peer counselling for middle school students experiencing family divorce: a deliberate psychological education model', *Elementary School Guidance and Counselling*, 26 (4), 279–94

Stacey, H. (1996), 'Mediation into schools does go', *Journal for Pastoral and Personal and Social Education*, 14 (2), 7–10

Stefani, L.A.J. (1994), 'Peer, self, and tutor assessment: Relative reliabilities', *Studies in Higher Education*, 19, 1, 69–75

Storm, A.M. (1991), 'Natural helpers: The differences in views of the male and female participants', *Research in Education*, October 1991 (EDRS Document).

Taylor, G. (1996), 'Creating a Circle of Friends' in Cowie, H. and Sharp, S. (eds) (1996), *Peer Counselling in schools: A Time to Listen*, London: David Fulton.

Whitaker, P., Barrett, J., Potter, M. and Thomson, G. (1998), 'Children with autism and peer group support: Using Circle of Friends', *British Journal of Special Education*, 25 (2), 60–64

Appendix 1

Further reading

Bradshaw, J. and Mayhew, E. (eds) (2005), *The Well-being of Children in the UK*, London: Save the Children

Bliss, T. and Tetley, J. (1996), *Circle Time: A Resource Book for Infant, Junior and Secondary Schools* (3rd edn), Bristol: Lame Duck Publishing

Geldard, K. and Geldard, D. (2001), *Working with Children in Small Groups: A Handbook for Counsellors, Educators and Community Workers*, Basingstoke: Palgrave

Greig, A. and Taylor, J. (1999), *Doing Research with Children*. London: Sage

Mason, M. and Dearden, J. (undated), *Snapshots of possibilities*, Alliance for Inclusive Education

National Children's Bureau (2004), *It's more than just listening! Children and young people talking about participation*, London: National Children's Bureau

Parsons, M. and Blake, S. (2004), *Peer support: an overview*, London: National Children's Bureau

Robinson, G. and Maines, B. (1997), *Crying for Help: The No Blame Approach to Bullying*, Bristol: Lucky Duck Publishing

Rue, Nanc. N. (1997), *Everything You Need to Know About Peer Mediation*, New York: Rosen Publishing Group

Save the Children (1999), *Right directions: a peer education resource introducing the UN Convention on the Rights of the Child*, London: Save the Children

Appendix 2

Government initiatives

Peer support as part of a wider commitment to young people's participation contributes in many ways to government strategies and initiatives across the United Kingdom particularly in the spheres of education, health, citizenship and social inclusion policies. With devolution these have been developed and implemented separately in each of the four regions and countries. Although the focus here is on English legislation and government initiatives, it is relevant to peer support work in the United Kingdom as a whole.

In 1991 the UK government signed up to the United Nations Convention on the Rights of the Child (UNCRC) (1989) which included articles 12 and 13 establishing the principle of young people having the right to participate in decisions that affect them. In 1997 the new Labour government identified social inclusion as a major policy priority and developed a wide range of initiatives targeting young people at risk of social exclusion. UNCRC along with The Children Act (CA)(2004), *Every Child Matters* (ECM) (DfES 2003) and the National Curriculum (NC) (DfEE/QCA 1999) provide the legal framework for youth participation, citizenship and social inclusion within which peer support programmes play a major role.

The ECM agenda is reflected in a range of key programmes set up to provide preventive services for children and young people at risk of social exclusion. These include:

- Sure Start www.surestart.gov.uk for infants aged 0 to 4;
- The Children's Fund www.childrensfund.gov.uk for children aged 5–13;
- Connexions www.connexions.gov.uk for teenagers aged 13–19.

Evans et al. (2006) point out that education issues and structures are also becoming central to the ECM agenda and give the example of the Extended Schools initiative delivering preventive services. The initiatives listed below can all utilize peer support in their implementation:

- *The Children Act 2004 and* Every Child Matters *(DfES 2003)* set out five national outcomes for children including 'making a positive contribution' and 'enjoying and achieving' where peer support practices make an important contribution.
- *The National Curriculum (DfEE/QCA 1999)* is founded on the stated belief in education as a route to the spiritual, social, physical and moral development of the individual. Its main aims provide a context for schools to develop peer support within their PSHE and citizenship curriculum.

- *The Children's Fund and Connexions* were launched in 2000 and 2001 respectively to provide services for children and young people aged five to 19. Both include peer support interventions as part of their services in schools.

- *Extended Schools*. As set out in the *Extended Schools* prospectus (DfES 2005a), the aim by 2010 is for all schools to provide access to a core offer of extended services. Within this context peer support projects could be part of a number of services promoting young people's confidence and constructive engagement and participation.

The Children Act 2004 and *Every Child Matters* 2003

The Every Child Matters: Change for Children programme (www.everychildmatters.gov.uk) aims to deliver whole system changes to children's services – locally and nationally. It provides a national framework of expectations and accountability in which 150 local authority-led change programmes operate to address local priorities for children, young people and families. The policies that have been developed to support this programme embody the government's principles of personalization, diverse provision, workforce reform, effective partnership working and autonomy for the front line. This approach to the well-being of children and young people from birth to age 19 places the goal of better child outcomes as central to all policies and young people's services.

The *Every Child Matters* framework born out of the Victoria Climbié Inquiry (Department of Health 2003) established a new direction and made an unassailable case for delivering radical improvement in opportunities and outcomes for children.

Key findings that underpin the *Every Child Matters* framework are:

▶ Widening gaps in outcomes are evident between socio-economic groups.
▶ Effects of disadvantage are early and have lasting consequences.
▶ Disadvantaged and 'at risk' young people are falling behind their peers.
▶ Services are often not working together sufficiently.
▶ The focus is on cure when it should be more on prevention.
▶ Child protection is not seen enough as the concern of everybody.

The Children Act provides the legislative spine for the *Every Child Matters: Change for Children programme*, which empowers the local and national changes to the system of children's services necessary to deliver:

- improved outcomes for children and young people
- a focus on narrowing gaps and opportunities for all
- support for parents, carers and families
- more focus on prevention, early identification and intervention
- integrated and personalized services
- better protection for children and young people.

The DfES emphasizes the importance of 'building a culture of participation' and refers to the work of the PK Research Consultancy and the National Children's Bureau (Kirby et al. 2003). It recommends the importance of:

- listening to young people so that their views bring about change
- identifying and illustrating the benefits of child and youth participation
- organizations thinking about how to create appropriate environments in which children and young people can be involved in meaningful ways, so that their views are listened to and acted upon
- organizations exploring how they can develop cultures and infrastructures which sustain and embed participation throughout all their activity.

Peer support projects as part of a wider package of measures in the PSHE and citizenship curriculum are an obvious and effective way to meet the above objectives and the five outcomes of The Children Act:

- Be Healthy
- Stay Safe
- Enjoy and Achieve
- Make a Positive Contribution
- Achieve Economic Well-being.

The role of peer support in implementing the *Every Child Matters* framework.

Be Healthy

This includes being healthy physically, mentally, emotionally and sexually as well as having a healthy lifestyle and choosing not to take harmful drugs. The National Healthy School Standard (NHSS 2004 and DfES/DoH 2005), and Healthy Care (NCB 2005) and The Healthy Schools Programme www.healthschools.gov.uk are programmes that are a key part of the government's drive to improve standards of health education. They also have young people's participation as the core element. They aim to make children, teachers, parents and communities more aware of the opportunities that exist in schools for improving health. Many schools have developed creative responses to the emotional needs of their students that include peer support programmes, (Chapter 10). Other programmes have brought about a reduction in self-harm and substance abuse (see Chapter 3). Hartley-Brewer (2002) refers to research showing that peer support programmes have resulted in: fewer students taking up (though not giving up) smoking; and increased practice of safe sex amongst certain groups.

By supporting their peers, students can promote emotional intelligence, emotional competence and emotional literacy, which are all essential to mental health as well as a crucial part of teaching and learning for staff and students in schools. Peer support promotes greater awareness among staff and students of issues that affect emotional health, such as bullying, exam pressure, racism, and peer and family relationships. Emotional problems and the needs of students are over represented in special schools and within exclusion statistics, and among adults with mental health problems. Hence the important role of peer support projects to support school students with special needs and those at risk of exclusion. Some examples are:

- Reflecting and problem solving around emotional needs where peer supporters use counselling skills (see Chapter 5) to work with others to understand and better meet their emotional and behavioural needs.

- Peer support as a gateway towards multi-agency working. Legislation plus national and local government initiatives confront agencies to work together more effectively in the interests of the most vulnerable and challenging students. Getting help from a peer supporter is often the first step for a troubled youngster and peer support services can direct students' paths to many agencies that offer help and support to young people with serious problems.

- Circle of Friends (see Chapter 7) where students work to problem solve and actively support the inclusion and behaviour change of one of their peers. This approach of reflecting about emotional and behavioural needs provides a deep level of problem solving for dealing with the most difficult to reach young people. Peers can work together, explore relationships, generate richer hypotheses about what is really going on underneath the behaviour of troubled students and by finding solutions and providing support can ensure greater inclusion of all students.

Stay Safe

This means that young people have security, stability and are cared for. It entails safety from: maltreatment, neglect, violence, sexual exploitation, accidental injury and death; bullying and discrimination; and crime and antisocial behaviour in and out of school. It also means young people growing up able to look after themselves. Informal peer support has been used by young people throughout history and is an example of the problem solving skills and positive peer relations that Evans et al. (2006) refer to as protective factors increasing resilience in young people. More formalized peer support strategies in schools can also promote safety such as:

- Peer mentoring (see Chapter 2) to help meet the needs of young people in schools and in public care.

- Peer counselling (see Chapter 2) to improve behaviour and reduce bullying and address emotional needs as older students offer active listening support and interventions.

- Cross age mentoring (see Chapter 2) where older students offer supportive. mentoring to younger pupils in the same school or in feeder primary schools.

- Peer mediation and conflict resolution (see Chapter 6) to resolve and restoring relationships without reliance on punishment.

- Circle of Friends (see above and Chapter 7).

- Community networks of support, creating student ownership of the solutions in local mainstream schools (see Chapters 2 and 10 for examples).

Enjoy and Achieve

This entails getting the most out of life and developing lifelong skills. In practice it means that all young people are ready for, attend and enjoy school where they achieve and stretch national education standards. They also achieve personal and social development and enjoy recreation. Peer support can play an important role in all of these aims and help create the inclusive classroom in mainstream school settings that is necessary for the enjoyment and achievement of all school students. As revealed in Chapter 3 research has shown that peer support projects can: increase confidence and self-esteem for both peer supporters and their clients; produce better academic performances; raise standards in mainstream curriculum;

and have a positive impact on disabled students. Projects can also help create a better atmosphere in schools and the wider community; enhance supportive pastoral systems; and promote greater student involvement in problem solving.

More examples of peer support promoting enjoyment and achievement in schools are:

- Peer education projects that enable inclusive teaching and learning (see Chapters 2 and 10) by diversifying/differentiating the curriculum; reflecting on attitudes to individual learning and the curriculum and challenging attitudes and mindsets.
- Welcoming new students with peer support for transition projects (see Chapters 5 and 10).
- The intentional building of relationships for example with Circle of Friends work.
- Peer support groups such as bereavement groups and peer education practices to combat isolated learning.

Make a Positive Contribution

This means developing the skills and attitudes for children and young people to contribute to the wider community in which they live. *Learning to Listen: Core principles for involving children and young people* (CYPU 2002) and *Working Together: Giving children and young people a say* (DfES 2004) are key documents making evident the English government's increasing commitment to young people's participation. All peer support projects by their very nature promote enterprising behaviour and involve students in decision making. They support the community and environment in various ways especially by encouraging students to be law-abiding and behave positively, choosing not to bully or discriminate. Central to peer support is the building of positive relationships and self-confidence so that young people can successfully deal with life changes and challenges.

Peer support is thus an important movement towards student participation and the journey towards adults listening to the powerful voice of young people. Local authorities are being encouraged to seek the views of young people in relation to the services they receive. Schools and the whole range of support services (for example, behaviour support, youth offending teams, social services and Child & Adolescent Mental Health Services (CAMHS) are being expected to routinely ask young people for their views). This goes beyond involving young people in plans that concern them such as care plans, individual education plans and pastoral support plans. Through peer support young people can be effectively engaged in giving their views through peer advocacy (see Chapter 2) and other models such as conflict resolution and mediation (see Chapter 6).

Achieve Economic Well-Being

This means having sufficient income and material necessities to be able to take up opportunities. It applies mostly to young people's lives beyond school, for example ensuring they engage in further education and/or are ready for employment or training after leaving. It means that young people live in decent homes and sustainable communities with access to transport and material goods to meet their basic needs. It also means living in households free from low income. Peer support cannot change economic circumstances outside school. However, it can make a vital contribution towards achieving future economic well-being by influencing young people's goals in life for the short and long term and equipping them to succeed. All the examples above of peer support projects helping students to 'enjoy and achieve', such as enhanced educational performance, will also contribute to their life chances and choices beyond school.

On a more practical note peer education programmes on handling money and finances can play an important role. Peer supporters themselves can benefit from improved communication and social skills that improve their future prospects (see Chapter 3). In addition peer supporters generate opportunities connected to their work. They can be involved in local and national conferences and workshops where their expenses are paid for, travel to places and have experiences they would not usually be able to afford financially. In some instances they can be paid for their work. Liverpool City Council pays its sixth-form mentors to reach performance targets on encouraging younger children to lose weight as part of a peer mentoring scheme (*Children Now* 2006). The valuable skills students learn in the peer support process are transferable to any situation in their future lives. Peer support is also affordable in schools and good value for money. Peer support is also cost-effective (see Chapter 3). Apart from the initial financial investment of setting up a peer support programme its maintenance is not expensive, as the primary resource is the young people themselves who are already present in school.

The National Curriculum

The National Curriculum (NC) aims for schools to: provide opportunities for all students to learn and achieve; and to promote students' spiritual, moral, social and cultural development and prepare all of them for the opportunities and responsibilities of life. These aims chime with the five outcomes of the Children Act and provide a vehicle for peer support projects.

What schools need to do to fulfil the requirements of the National Curriculum (National Children's Bureau 2006a):

- Develop the knowledge and understanding of their students' own and different beliefs.
- Ensure students understand their rights and responsibilities.
- Develop students' integrity and autonomy in promoting respect for their environments and communities; develop self-esteem and emotional development.
- Help students form and maintain satisfying relationships.

The full range of peer support as outlined in Chapter 2 can play a central role in achieving the aims of the NC by working within each of the following strands for delivery of the NC non-statutory framework for PSHE and citizenship at all Key Stages:

- Developing students' confidence and responsibility and maximizing their abilities.
- Preparing them to play an active role as citizens.
- Enabling them to develop a healthier, safer lifestyle.
- Helping them develop good relationships and respect the differences between people.

At Key Stages 3 and 4 citizenship is a foundation subject in the NC and peer support projects can be part of the delivery in three further strands:

- Knowledge and understanding of becoming informed citizens.
- Developing skills of enquiry and communication.
- Developing skills of participation and responsible action.

Peer support can help schools meet the statutory requirements of 'National Curriculum Citizenship at KS3 & KS4' (DfEE/QCA 1999) and enhance it (QCA 1999) in a variety of ways such as peers accurately assessing each other (Stefani 1994). Peer support can also help schools meet other legislation especially in relation to certain aspects of PSHE such as sex and relationship education, drugs, pupil participation and financial capability (see Appendix 3 for a list of websites with policy documents and guidance on these and others). A good example is the APAUSE peer sex education programme in schools that also contributes to the government's strategy for reducing teenage pregnancy (see Chapters 2 and 9).

The Children's Fund and Connexions

The Children's Fund established in 2000 aims to develop services that support multi-agency working for preventive services for children aged five to 13 years who are at risk of social exclusion. Connexions, launched in 2001, is a universal support service for 13 to 19 year olds, delivered by local teams of personal advisers. Both service providers build on the protective work of Sure Start launched in 1998 for deprived infants aged 0 to 4.

Peer support interventions funded by the Children's Fund must be in schools in socially deprived areas and focus on those children 'most at risk of social exclusion through poverty and disadvantage' (CYPU 2002). An example of such an initiative is the Staffordshire Children's Fund Peer Support Project in two high schools and two of their feeder primary schools (see Chapter 8).

Although Connexions was launched as a universal service, its primary goal is to address the multi-dimensional problems faced by young people at risk of social exclusion. Peer support projects are an example of the kinds of services with which Connexions can become involved through the personal advisers who work in schools.

Extended Schools

Launched in 25 local authorities in 2002, extended schools are one of the key mechanisms for implementing the ECM agenda. The National Remodelling Team (NRT) was appointed in 2005 to support local authorities and schools in taking extended services forward to fit local circumstances. Clearly peer support projects would not be relevant in every extended service but they could play an important role in any service promoting increased participation and achievements of young people.

Emerging policies

The Government's Education White Paper, 'Higher Standards, Better Schools for All' (DfES 2005b) proposed legislation to establish Trust Schools and Academies with considerable control over their own admissions. At the time of writing it is now the controversial Education and Inspections Bill (DfES 2006b). Some changes made since the White Paper was first published have allayed some fears over selection and admissions policies. Some aspects of the Bill are congruent with the ideas underpinning peer support, such as:

- Personalized learning and emotional literacy.

- The duty imposed on governing bodies of all schools to have regard to the views of the local authority's Children and Young People's Plan.

- New powers for authorities to make arrangements to enable them to establish the identities of children in their area who are not receiving a suitable education which is vital to ensure that 'every child matters' within a local authority area.

- New partnerships between schools thus creating further possibilities for peer support to be part of improving attainment and opportunities for young people.

Appendix 3

Resources

Organizations

The Anti-Bullying Alliance www.ncb.org.uk/aba

Anti-bullying Network www.antibullying.net/

APAUSE www.programmes.ex.ac.uk/apause/index2.htm

Association for Citizenship Teaching (ACT) www.teachingcitizenship.co.uk

Beatbullying www.beatbullying.org

Black Health Agency www.blackhealthagency.org.uk

Bullyfreeworld www.bullyfreeworld.co.uk

Co-counselling International www.co-counselling.org.uk

Childhood Bereavement Network www.childhoodbereavementnetwork.org.uk

Childline www.childline.org.uk

Childline in Partnership with Schools (CHIPS) www.childline.org.uk/Schools.asp

Children & Young People's Unit Website www.cypu.gov.uk/corporate/home.cfm

Children Now www.childrennow.co.uk

Children in Wales – Plant Yng Nghymru www.childreninwales.org.uk/index.html

Children's Legal Centre www.childrenslegalcentre.com

Child Trends www.childtrends.org

The Chinese Youth Forum www.cyf.org.uk

Department of Education and Skills www.standards.dfes.gov.uk

Disability Equality in Education (DEE) www.diseed.org.uk

Drug Education Forum drugeducation.org.uk

The Hansard Society – HeadsUp www.headsup.org.uk

Inclusive Solutions www.inclusive-solutions.com/circlesoffriends.asp

Jenny Mosley Consultancies & Positive Press Ltd www.circle-time.co.uk

Kidscape www.kidscape.org.uk

Leap Confronting Conflict and the Young Mediators' Network (YMN) www.leaplinx.com

Let's Talk Sex www.channel4.com/letstalksex

Mediation UK www.mediationuk.org.uk

The Mental Health foundation www.mentalhealth.org.uk

Mentoring and Befriending Foundation www.mandbf.org.uk

The National Children's Bureau www.ncb.org.uk

National Society for the Prevention of Cruelty to Children www.nspcc.org.uk

The Northern Ireland Assembly www.niassembly.gov.uk/ www.allchildrenni.gov.uk

Northern Ireland Youth Forum www.niyf.org/home.cfm

The Office of the Children's Commissioner www.childrenscommissioner.org

Participation works www.participationworks.org.uk

Peer Counsellor Journal www.mentors.ca/PCJ12.1PRN.html,

Peer Support Networker peersupport.ukobservatory.com

Peer Support Works www.peersupportworks.co.uk

The Quaker Peace Education Project www.peacemakers.org.uk

Qualifications and Curriculum Authority www.qca.org.uk

Safeguarding children in education www.teachernet.gov.uk/childprotection

Save The Children UK www.scfuk.org.uk

School Councils UK www.schoolcouncils.org

Scottish Youth Parliament www.scottishyouthparliament.org.uk

Sex Education Forum www.ncb.org.uk/sef

Teachers' TV www.teachers.tv

Trust for the Study of Adolescence www.studyofadolescence.org.uk

UK Youth Parliament www.ukyp.org.uk/4655/index.html

Welsh Assembly www.wales.gov.uk/subichildren/toc-e.htm

Wired for Health www.wiredforhealth.gov.uk

Women's Aid www.thehideout.org.uk

Working with Men www.workingwithmen.org

YoungGov www.direct.gov.uk/youngpeople

Young Voice www.young-voice.org

Accreditation providers

ASDAN (www.asdan.org.uk) is an approved awarding body offering programmes and qualifications to develop key skills and life skills. Its Certificate of Personal Effectiveness (CoPE) at levels 1, 2 and 3 (www.asdan.org.uk/cope_award) is the qualification wrapper for ASDAN's Bronze, Silver, Gold, and Universities Awards, FE Awards and Short Course awards, is now approved as a full qualification, following QCA's evaluation of the pilot project with 200 schools and colleges throughout the UK. This means that, as from September 2005, all centres registered with ASDAN can use CoPE, once they have undertaken appropriate training (see below), and then count the qualification as a GCSE equivalent in their Performance Table returns to the DfES. CoPe Staff Development Workshops (www.asdan.org.uk/cope_workshops) are registered centres that can access information and support materials in the secure area and purchase materials.

Edexcel (www.edexcel.org.uk/quals/) offer routes to accreditation as follows: Key Skills (Skills for Life); GNVQ, Citizenship Studies (www.edexcel.org.uk/subjects/a-z/citizenship); Certificate in Life Skills (Citizenship & Community Studies) and a GCSE (Short Course) in Citizenship Studies.

The National Open College Network (NOCN) (www.nocn.org.uk) is a provider of accreditation services for people aged from 14 and over. It provides national qualifications and programmes in a wide range of subject areas involving the kinds of skills taught in peer support training courses and offers a local accreditation service, through the OCNs, that provides recognition of achievement through the award of credit.

Appendix 4

Monitoring and evaluation

What follows are photocopiable examples of questionnaires and review sheets together with examples of analysis and collation of data. Sections 1 and 2 are examples of before and after questionnaires designed to find out attitude changes among participants of a training course (also see Cowie and Sharp 1996, pages 140–141 for useful questions and Scherer-Thompson 2003, for more examples). Section 3 shows how the data from the pre- and post- questionnaires can be analysed. Sections 5 and 6 are review sheets for peer mentors and Year 7 students to complete after experiencing the service for a school term. Finally section 7 is an example of how data can be collated from service user review sheets (based on a project which involved three schools in one town).

1. Pre-course questionnaire

Name of school: ....

Name of student: .... Date: ....

Date of birth: .... Mum's first name: ....

Tick: ○ Male   ○ Female   ○ Asian   ○ Black   ○ White   ○ Dual/Mixed heritage

How much do you agree with the following statements?
Tick whether you strongly agree (SA), agree (A), don't know (DK), disagree (D) or strongly disagree (SD)

		1	2	3	4	5
0	We should always try to help each other	SA	A	DK	D	SD
1	If someone else is unhappy it is not my job to help	SA	A	DK	D	SD
2	On the whole I am happy with the way I am	SA	A	DK	D	SD
3	We should sort out our own friendship problems	SA	A	DK	D	SD
4	If I see someone bullied and do nothing about it my behaviour is almost as bad as the bully's	SA	A	DK	D	SD
5	Talking with someone about home problems can help	SA	A	DK	D	SD
6	Most of the time I am confident	SA	A	DK	D	SD
7	We should sort out our own schoolwork problems	SA	A	DK	D	SD
8	Talking with someone about friendship problems can help	SA	A	DK	D	SD
9	We should sort out our own home problems	SA	A	DK	D	SD
10	I am able to do lots of things well	SA	A	DK	D	SD
11	Talking with someone about schoolwork problems can help	SA	A	DK	D	SD
12	I feel that I am part of a group of friends	SA	A	DK	D	SD
13	Have the chance to make new friends with others	SA	A	DK	D	SD
14	Improve my existing friendships with other children	SA	A	DK	D	SD

		1	2	3	4	5
15	Help other children	SA	A	DK	D	SD
16	Develop more confidence	SA	A	DK	D	SD
17	Learn listening and co-counselling skills and/or mediation skills	SA	A	DK	D	SD
18	Have a chance to open up more about my feelings and thoughts	SA	A	DK	D	SD
19	Learn more about myself and others	SA	A	DK	D	SD
20	Improve my relationships with my family	SA	A	DK	D	SD
21	Have a chance to play games	SA	A	DK	D	SD
22	Work in groups	SA	A	DK	D	SD

Other comments (please write below anything else that sums up why you think it will be a good idea to do the training):

2. Post-course questionnaire

Name of school: ....

Name of student: .... Date: ....

Date of birth: .... Mum's first name: ....

Tick: ○ Male   ○ Female   ○ Asian   ○ Black   ○ White   ○ Dual/Mixed heritage

How much do you agree with the following statements?
Tick whether you strongly agree (SA), agree (A), don't know (DK), disagree (D) or strongly disagree (SD)

		1	2	3	4	5
0	We should always try to help each other	SA	A	DK	D	SD
1	If someone else is unhappy it is not my job to help	SA	A	DK	D	SD
2	On the whole I am happy with the way I am	SA	A	DK	D	SD
3	We should sort out our own friendship problems	SA	A	DK	D	SD
4	If I see someone bullied and do nothing about it my behaviour is almost as bad as the bully's	SA	A	DK	D	SD
5	Talking with someone about home problems can help	SA	A	DK	D	SD
6	Most of the time I am confident	SA	A	DK	D	SD
7	We should sort out our own schoolwork problems	SA	A	DK	D	SD
8	Talking with someone about friendship problems can help	SA	A	DK	D	SD
9	We should sort out our own home problems	SA	A	DK	D	SD
10	I am able to do lots of things well	SA	A	DK	D	SD
11	Talking with someone about schoolwork problems can help	SA	A	DK	D	SD
12	I feel that I am part of a group of friends	SA	A	DK	D	SD
13	Have the chance to make new friends with others	SA	A	DK	D	SD
14	Improve my existing friendships with other children	SA	A	DK	D	SD

		1	2	3	4	5
15	Help other children	SA	A	DK	D	SD
16	Develop more confidence	SA	A	DK	D	SD
17	Learn listening and co-counselling and/or mediation skills	SA	A	DK	D	SD
18	Have a chance to open up more about my feelings and thoughts	SA	A	DK	D	SD
19	Learn more about myself and others	SA	A	DK	D	SD
20	Improve my relationships with my family	SA	A	DK	D	SD
21	Have a chance to play games	SA	A	DK	D	SD
22	Work in groups	SA	A	DK	D	SD

Other comments (please write below anything else that sums up why you think it will be a good idea to do the training):

3. An example of an analysis of the data from pre- and post-course questionnaires (sections 1 and 2)

The raw data from the completed questionnaires in four secondary schools was converted manually into tables on Microsoft Excel, which in turn were converted into tables showing the amount of positive and negative movement as well as no change: 44.41 per cent of the responses of 68 students to the total of 1,496 questions showed overall improvement; 46.35 per cent showed overall no change; and 9.23 per cent showed overall negative movement. Bearing in mind the trainees were chosen for their positive attitudes it is not surprising that nearly half showed no overall change and that a slightly smaller proportion showed positive movement after the three day course. The relatively small percentage of negative responses was also to be expected bearing in mind the challenging nature of the course. To find out how many students showed significant change beyond mere chance a basic sign test was applied. A score of 16 or more positive movements for a respondent answering 22 questions indicated a significant improvement. Such a change was shown by 17.65 per cent of 68 respondents. Their scores were calculated by adding their positive responses and subtracting negative responses. Again this result was hardly surprising when taking into consideration their positive predisposition. Although the test was reassuring in that it showed that the course led to a trend in significant overall positive change, it was more useful in revealing which items showed the most and least movement and points the way for changes in the course. The data could be further analysed using factor analysis and a control group alongside the trainee group before the next set of training courses and after the respondents have been working on their project for a term.

4. Buddy Room referral form   (Designed by a student at Hagley Park Sports College)

To	
Student	
Buddy(s)		

☐ Urgent   ☐ To inform you   ☐ Wants to see you

Date of incident		Today's date	
Location			
Time of incident		Time now	

Statement (Use extra paper if needed)

Signed by:

Student	
Buddy(s)		

5. Review of being a peer mentor/mediator from date–date

School: .... Age: ....

Tick: ○ Male   ○ Female   ○ Asian   ○ Black   ○ White   ○ Dual/Mixed heritage

What I have gained so far from being a peer mentor/mediator to Year 7 children/disputants:

What I think the Year 7 children/disputants have gained so far:

What has been difficult about being a peer mentor/mediator:

What has been easy about being a peer mentor/mediator:

Tick below what you found useful on the peer mentor training days:

1. Opening and closing circles.
2. Listening skills
3. Counselling techniques, for example, validations and directions
4. Co-counselling in pairs
5. Support groups
6. Introducing yourself to the group
7. Games
8. Show and tells
9. Confidentiality
10. Discharging and expressing your feelings
11. Learning about intelligence and behaviour patterns
12. Anti-bullying awareness raising
13. The young people's commitment
14. Appreciation sheets

Tick below what you did not find useful on the peer mentor training days:

1. Opening and closing circles
2. Listening skills
3. Counselling techniques, for example, validations and directions
4. Co-counselling in pairs
5. Support groups
6. Introducing yourself to the group
7. Games
8. Show and tells
9. Confidentiality
10. Discharging and expressing your feelings
11. Learning about intelligence and behaviour patterns
12. Anti-bullying awareness raising
13. The young people's commitment
14. Appreciation sheets

My ideas for future improvements to the service:

6. Year 7 students'/disputants' review of the peer support service

School: .... Age: ....

Tick: ○ Male   ○ Female   ○ Asian   ○ Black   ○ White   ○ Dual/Mixed heritage

1. **What have you liked so far about having the peer mentors'/mediators' drop-in service? (please tick yes or no to the following):**

	yes	no
a. It was a useful service for us to have		
b. I do not think it was necessary for us to have it		
c. I used it and found the mentors/mediators helpful		
d. I used it and did not find it helpful		
e. I didn't use but it was good to know it was there just in case		
f. I didn't use it even if I had a problem		
g. Other (please write below)		

h. If I didn't use it, that is because:

i. I think it could be improved by: (please write any ideas below)

        Peer Support Works: a step by step guide to long term success

2. What did you gain from having the peer mentors in your tutor group? (please tick yes or no to the following):

	yes	no
a. The chance to make friends with older students		
b. Developing more confidence with older students		
c. Learning some listening and co-counselling skills		
d. A chance to open up more about my feelings and thoughts		
e. Learning more about myself and others		
f. Improving my friendships with the other children in my class		
g. A chance to play games		
h. Working in small groups		

i. Other (please write what it is below)

j. Did you dislike any of the mentoring activities in your class? If so write below which you found difficult from the above list a–i

7. Presentation of collated data collected from service user reviews

Three high schools from one town: Year 7 reviews of their peer mentoring services 2005

A total of 343 Year 7 students from three schools filled in the reviews. These were 172 males and 171 females. Of these two girls were Asian, four girls were black and eight boys and four girls were mixed heritage. They came from the following schools:

School 1: 93 male (88 white and 5 mixed heritage) and 88 female (82 white, two Asian, two black and two mixed heritage) students

School 2: 65 male (62 white and three mixed heritage) and 73 female (69 white, two black and two mixed heritage) students

School 3: 14 male and 10 female white students in two Year 7 nurture groups group

The percentage of students indicating what they had gained from having the peer mentors in their group over the past year is as follows:

73% – A chance to play games.

67% – Learning more about myself and others.

66% – Improving my friendships with the other children in my class.

64% – The chance to make friends with older students.

63% – Working in small groups.

62% – A chance to open up more about my feelings and thoughts.

61% – Developing more confidence with older students.

42% – Learning some listening and co-counselling skills.

Other comments and gains cited by a few individual girls on the mentoring activities
as follows: 'They were all fun'; 'A chance to talk about bullying openly'; 'They were really helpful'; 'They help you find the rooms where to go'; 'A lot more confidence'; 'Building confidence'; 'Team work'; 'Improved speaking and listening'; 'Confident to talk to other students'; 'I got to show things off from home in class'; and 'I got to see things that other people in class brought in'.

Some individual girls commented on what mentoring activities they disliked as follows:
'It was rubbish'; 'They could listen more'; 'I didn't get it'; 'I didn't like the quizzes – they're difficult'; 'Listening to people is sometimes hard' ; 'It was boring'; 'Circle time'; 'To work in small groups'; 'Didn't like any of them'; 'When the boys wouldn't listen'; 'Some games were pointless because we didn't learn anything from them' ; 'Some games were fun and some weren't'; and 'Making friends with older students was difficult'.

Some individual boys commented on mentoring activities they disliked as follows:
'I found it difficult to meet new friends in the form. Because I have no friends in the form'
'I didn't like xxxxxx. She had a go at us constantly'; 'Giving up my feelings' 'the bullying awareness was not difficult'; and 'The mentors are sexist in games and blackmail us'.

Appendix 5

Conflict resolution

What follows are photocopiable handouts to accompany the conflict resolution training course in Chapter 6.

Handout 1

Conflict situations where peer mediators can help

Peer mediators are best placed to deal with low level disputes such as: alleged theft from a student; name calling; low level bullying; 'play' arguments; teasing; attention seeking behaviour; friends falling out; relationship arguments; rumour-spreading; and ostracizing. These types of disputes can develop into much greater conflicts when they give rise to students gathering together allies, and seeking revenge. Without early intervention, these may lead to long-lasting disruption of a high degree. Peer mediators are well placed to spot these disputes in their early stages and to intervene by applying their skills in a mediation service. If not dealt with early on, disputes can develop into more serious bullying which can be emotionally or physically harmful behaviour such as: abusive name calling; taunting; mocking; making offensive comments; kicking; hitting; pushing; taking belongings; text messaging; emailing; malicious gossiping; excluding people from groups; and spreading hurtful and untruthful rumours. Bullying behaviour can be repetitive, wilful or persistent; intentionally harmful; carried out by an individual or a group; creating an imbalance of power leaving the victim feeling defenceless. Peer mediators can help with most of these forms of bullying if both parties are willing but would need to refer serious physical bullying to adults.

Conflict situations where peer mediators will need to refer to adults

Physical assault in schools cannot be tolerated and there is little room for peer mediation here. Adults in schools will need to deal with violent conflict such as hitting, punching, tripping, spitting, hair pulling, use of weapons, gang fights and other forms of physical fighting and/or bullying. After these have been dealt with, usually with sanctions, peer mediation can be used to rebuild relationships between disputants.

Racial, sexual, homophobic and disability harassment cannot be tolerated and although peer mediators can help in non-violent situations they are best used to rebuild relationships after sanctions have taken place. Bullying often takes the form of racism, sexism, homophobia and disability harassment. However, in all cases it is important to check that the conflict is not a straightforward dispute between students who just happen to be from different racial backgrounds, genders, abilities or sexual orientation and is not directly or indirectly related to those differences. A fine line separates bullying from racist, sexist, homophobic and disability harassment and it is difficult but important to distinguish between them. Bullying is behaviour that is intentionally hurtful in the ways listed above but is not necessarily based on attacking a person's unchangeable identity. It becomes racist, sexist, homophobic and/or disability harassment when it is an attack on a person's fundamental identity which is a more serious form of aggression. We need to be aware that some students do not realize their behaviour is bullying, racist, sexist, homophobic or disability harassment and most will claim that to be the case. In any conflict, especially that involving bullying or identity harassment, there is inherently an imbalance of power between white and minority ethnic disputants, between males and females, between heterosexual, homosexual and bisexual disputants, or between able-bodied and disabled disputants. This is due to the nature of our racist, sexist, homophobic and able-bodyist society and must be taken into account and addressed by mediators to maintain equity.

Handout 2

The Maligned Wolf (Bodine et al. 1994)

I lived in the forest. It was my home and I cared for it. I tried to keep it neat and clean.

One lovely sunny day, while I was clearing up some litter left behind by picnickers, I heard footsteps. As I peeped from behind a tree I saw a little girl picking flowers in a clearing away from the path. She was carrying a basket. I was immediately suspicious because she wasn't on the path, she was trampling on my flowers and was dressed so strangely, all in red, with her head covered up as if she didn't want to be recognized.

Now I know that we shouldn't judge people by what they wear, but she was in my forest and I felt I ought to find out more about her. I asked her who she was, where she came from – you know, that kind of thing. At first she said all primly that she didn't speak to strangers. I was very upset I could tell you. Me a stranger! In my own forest! Well really! After all I'd brought up my whole family in that forest. Then she told me it was no business of mine where she was going and tried to push past. She did calm down a bit and told me some story about going to visit her sick grandmother and taking her a basket of lunch. She appeared to be a basically honest person but I did think she should learn better manners and that it is inconsiderate to barge through someone's home suspiciously and unsuitably dressed.

I let her go on her way, but ran on ahead to her grandmother's house. She is actually a friend of mine and she is a very nice lady. When I saw her I explained what had happened and how I felt, and she agreed that her granddaughter needed to learn a little more consideration. We planned that I would pretend to be her in bed with her bedclothes on so I could tell her granddaughter what she had done wrong. Granny agreed to stay out of sight until I called her – actually she hid in the next room.

When the girl arrived I invited her into the bedroom where I was in bed. She came in all rosy cheeked and then made a personal remark about my ears. I've been insulted before, so I made the best of it by suggesting that my big ears would help me to hear better. What I meant by that was that I liked her and wanted to pay close attention to what she was saying. But she then made another clever remark about my bulging eyes. Now you can understand how I was beginning to feel about this little girl who put up such a nice front, but underneath was a very unpleasant person! Still I've made a practice of turning the other cheek, so all I said was that my big eyes helped me to see her better.

However, she still wasn't finished. Her next remark really got to me. I've got this problem with having big teeth and that little girl actually drew my attention to them. I know I should have better self-control, but I leapt up from the bed growling that my teeth would help me eat her better!

Now let's face it, no wolf is going to ever eat a little girl. Everyone knows that, but the silly child started running around the house screaming. I followed her, trying to calm her down. I took her grandmother's clothes off, but that seemed to make it worse. Then all of a sudden the door burst open and a six-foot forestry commission ranger was standing there with an axe in his hand! I looked at him and realized that I was in real trouble. There was an open window behind me so out I went.

I'd like to say that was the end of it, but her grandmother never explained my side of the story. Before long the word got about that I was a horrid untrustworthy creature. I don't know about that little girl in the funny red outfit, but I certainly haven't lived happily ever after!

Handout 3

Conflict management styles (source: Lloyd 2000)

Withdrawing (The turtle). Turtles withdraw into their shells to avoid conflict. They give up their personal goals and relationships. They stay away from the issues and from the people with whom they are in conflict. They feel helpless, believe it is hopeless to try and resolve the conflict and find it easier to withdraw physically and psychologically than to face it. By avoiding or denying the conflict, such a person hopes the problem will go away. Usually it doesn't. So, this is not a useful approach.

Smoothing (The teddy bear). Teddy bears value their relationships more than their goals. They want to be accepted and liked by others. They believe conflicts should be avoided in favour of harmony and that people cannot discuss conflicts without damaging relationships. They are afraid people will get hurt and relationships will be ruined if the conflict continues so they give up on their goals and try to smooth over the problems. Many teddy bears prefer to give in rather than fight. Sometimes they are being a martyr, sometimes scared, sometimes seeking appreciation, and so on. In any case, this is another unhelpful approach, because it is unfair, it generates no creative solutions and usually such an accommodator remains very unhappy.

Forcing (The shark). Sharks try to overpower opponents by forcing them to accept their solution to a conflict. Their goals are more important to them than their relationships. They are unconcerned about the needs of others and seek their own goals at any cost. They assume conflicts are settled by one side winning and the other losing and they want to be the winner. Winning makes them feel proud and an achiever whereas losing makes them feel weak, inadequate and a failure. They try to win by attacking, overwhelming and intimidating others. Some sharks get mad and blame the other person and such a conflict becomes an ugly battle in which they must win at any cost. This is an approach that causes more harm than good because it stops all constructive thinking, is unfair and produces lasting hostility.

Compromising (The fox). Foxes are moderately concerned about their own goals and their relationships with others. They seek to give up part of their goals and persuade the other person to give up part of theirs – a compromise. They seek the middle ground and are willing to sacrifice part of what they want in order to reach an agreement for the common good. That would be wonderful, if it were entirely true, but sometimes a part of this approach is subtle but deftly trying to win more ground than your opponent. The objective becomes trying to prove you are clever or slick. Thus, political or social pressure, misrepresentation, threats-with-a-smile, and so on may slip in, rather than simply seeking an optimal solution for both sides.

Confronting (The owl). Owls highly value their own goals and their relationships. They see a conflict as a problem to be solved and seek a solution that achieves their own goals and those of the other person. They see conflicts as ways of improving relationships by reducing tension. By seeking resolutions that satisfy both sides owls maintain a good relationship and are not satisfied until a solution is found and the tensions have been resolved. A few people can control their anger, and competitive and defeatist feelings and genuinely seek an innovative, fair, optimal solution for both parties. This creative, integrative and win-win approach is obviously the most useful.

Handout 4

Questionnaire (source: Lloyd 2000)

When you are working with other people on a problem of theirs, how often do the following occur? Mark each behaviour with the following score:

Very often   – 4
Often   – 3
Occasionally   – 2
Almost never   – 1
Never   – 0

Generally unhelpful behaviours   **Generally helpful behaviours**

Not listen ___   Listen actively ___

Hurry them up ___   Give them time to think ___

Tell them what to do ___   Balance emotion and reason ___

Take sides ___   Check how people are feeling ___

Make decisions for them ___   Involve people in discussions ___

Hold back useful information ___   Provide a realistic focus ___

Make promises you can't keep ___   Discuss rules openly ___

Compare your experience to theirs ___   Disclose all relevant information ___

Devalue their experience ___   Maintain fairness and respect ___

Make assumptions ___   Check your own assumptions ___

Adopt a superior tone ___   Ask their opinions and advice ___

Forget pieces of information ___   Ask for their guidance on how to help and make things easier ___

Talk inappropriately about yourself ___

Handout 5

Prompt sheets for mediators

Introductions
Mediators introduce themselves and explain what they do.

What mediators do

- Mediators listen to you.

- Mediators don't take sides.

- Mediators don't tell you what to do.

- Mediators help you make up your mind about what to do.

- Mediators keep secrets unless they are about someone getting seriously harassed or something illegal.

Check that both parties want to mediate
If they do, introduce the rules and check they agree with them (or ask them to sign an agreement).

The rules of mediation
You must agree to keep everything said confidential and if you break this you will be referred to a teacher. Tell your clients the following rules:

- You must accept our leadership as mediators.

- You must agree not to fight.

- You must not use bad language or name-calling.

- You must not use put-downs.

- You must not interrupt the other person.

- You must not blame the other person.

- You must be as honest as you can and do your best to solve the problem.

- You must agree that the mediator must share with adult supervisors anything discussed concerning suicide, child abuse, racial, sexual, homophobic or disability harassment, illegal drugs or weapons on the school grounds.

Mediation process

Get Party 1 to tell her/his story.

You repeat the main points back.

Get Party 2 to tell her/his story.

You repeat the main points back.

Ask Party 1 how s/he felt.

You repeat the feelings.

Ask Party 2 how s/he felt.

You repeat the feelings.

Ask Party 1 if s/he understands how Party 2 felt.

Ask Party 2 if s/he understands how Party 1 felt.

Ask Party 1 what s/he needs to happen to solve the problem.

Ask Party 2 what s/he needs to happen to solve the problem.

Try to get an agreement.

Summarize the agreement and ask them to write it down and shake hands on it.

Offer a follow-up session if they want it.

Handout 6

Examples of role-play situations

- Jason/Jill a Year 7 student since starting the school in September spent most of the time with two best friends from primary school. However, they started spending time with another group and didn't want to be friends with J anymore. J feels very upset and lonely and feels that everyone else has their groups of friends and J is left out. J still tries to be with them during break and lunchtimes but they keep telling J to go away. It makes J angry and J blames the other friends and complains about them to other students. J doesn't want to come to school and would prefer to stay at home if J's mum would allow it. One of the friends, Lenny/Liz, has complained to the tutor that J has been spreading nasty rumours about the new friends so the tutor arranged for J and L to go to peer mediation.

- Tim/Tracey is in Year 10. There are some students smoking cigarettes around the corner from the school, all T's friends are smoking and T's best friend Mick/Michelle is pressurizing T to join in. T is afraid they'll exclude T from the group if T doesn't, had a big row with M about it and threatens to tell the teachers about the smokers. They both decide to go to the peer mediators to sort it out.

- Sean/Sadia is in Year 8 and small for his/her age. It feels like everyone in year 8 is laughing at S because of S's short stature. One student in particular called Billy/Bushra keeps calling S 'titch' and other names which S doesn't like. S tried to ignore it but was getting very upset and didn't know what to do about it so asked the mediators if they would sort it out with B. They asked B to have a mediation session with S and B agreed.

- Harry/Halima in Year 9 is very angry with H's friend, Steve/Shiren, for going out with H's ex so soon after they split up and suspects s/he was being two-timed. H feels she can never forgive S for this and has started spreading rumours about S. This has resulted in S being shut out from their friendship group.

- Afraz/Amy is 16 in the spring term of Year 11 and the exams are coming up. A didn't do very well in the mock exams before Christmas and A's parents are nagging as well as the teachers. A is behind with coursework and feels panicky and hopeless about the whole thing. Noreena/Nathan has got a job lined up for when N leaves and can't understand why A's making such a fuss, and wants them to go out much more than they do. N says they should finish if A doesn't lighten up and has agreed to go to mediation with A to sort things out.

Handout 7

What to say in difficult situations (source: Britton 2000)

In difficult situations look at the person, call her/him by her/his name and say any of the following.

When a disputant continually interrupts:

- She listened to you say what happened and I need you to listen to her now.

- I would like you to stop interrupting, as agreed. I promise you will have another chance to talk as soon as she finishes.

- I can see it's important for you to be heard and you will get your turn when she's finished.

- I'm getting annoyed when you interrupt because you're not giving her time to talk.

- I feel frustrated when you interrupt because we are trying to help you solve your problem.

- These interruptions show that you are not ready to mediate now so I'm stopping the session. Do you want to try another time or would you rather take the problem to one of the teachers?

When disputants insult or name call each other:

- You agreed to no name calling.

- Say what you feel but use respectful language.

- I don't want you to call him names as it might make him not want to solve the problem.

- I feel frustrated when you call her names as it holds us back from resolving this problem.

- These insults show that you are not ready to mediate now so I'm stopping the session. Do you want to try another time or would you rather take the problem to one of the teachers?

When one or both disputants call the other a liar:

- You may think that but if you keep saying it that might not help to solve the situation.

- You don't seem happy with what she just said.

- There seems to have been a misunderstanding.

- I get confused when I hear two different versions of what happened. Can you both help me out here?

- I can understand how you both might see the situation differently.

- Calling each other liars all the time shows that you are not ready to mediate now so I'm stopping the session. Do you want to try another time or would you rather take the problem to one of the teachers?

When one or both disputants will not talk:

- This mediation session won't work if both of you don't use the chance to speak and be heard.

- It doesn't seem as if you are ready to mediate. Do you want to try another time?

- You seem upset. If you like we can stop this session and mediate another time. Would you like this, yes or no?

When one of the disputants begins to cry:

- It's OK to cry. We can pause for a short while.

- I can see you're upset. I can see there's a problem. You're right this is a real problem.

- Since you're upset we could stop for a few minutes so you can get yourself together.

- You seem very upset. Would you like to continue after a break or postpone the session till later?

When one of the disputants gets out of her/his seat and moves around:

- I feel frustrated when you get of your seat as it disturbs the session and we can't sort out the problem.

- When you get out of your seat, it really disrupts the session. Please sit down so we can continue.

- You getting out of your seat shows that you are not ready to mediate now so I'm stopping the session. Do you want to try another time or would you rather get help from a teacher?

Acknowledgements

Page 165 Handout 2 'The Maligned Wolf' adapted from 'The Story of Little Red Riding Hood and the Wolf, Retold Through Negotiation', from Crawford, D. and Bodine, R., *Conflict Resolution Education: A Guide to Implementing Programs in Schools, Youth-Serving Organizations, and Community and Juvenile Justice Settings; Program Report, NCJ 160935. OJJDP, October 1996, pp xv – xvi.* Reproduced with permission from the United States Department of Justice.

Page 166 Handout 3 'Conflict management styles' from Lloyd, K. (2000), *OCN Introduction to Community Mediation Skills*, Wolverhampton Mediation Service pp 24-5

Page 167 Handout 4 'Questionnaire' from Lloyd, K. (2000), *OCN Introduction to Community Mediation Skills*, Wolverhampton Mediation Service, page 57

Page 171 Handout 7 'What to say in difficult situations' from Britton, F. (2000), *Active Citizenship: a teaching toolkit*, CSV Education for Citizenship, London: Hodder and Stoughton, 140–41

Photographs of students from:
Hagley Park Sports College, Rugeley, Staffordshire
Longton High School, Stoke-on-Trent, Staffordshire
Rising Brook High School, Stafford,Staffordshire
Wilnecote High School, Tamworth, Staffordshire
Wolstanton High School, Newcastle-under-Lyme, Staffordshire.

Index

Data Protection Act 118
Demetriades, A. 12
diversity 86

economic well-being 144–145
Education and Inspections Bill (2006)
 146–147
Elton Report (1989) 12
email services 22, 23, 129
emotions 42, 60, 81–82, 142–143
empathy 59–60, 78–79, 165
empowerment 23–24, 28, 29, 128
enjoyment 143–144
evaluation *see* monitoring and evaluation
Evans, R. et al. 140, 143
Every Child Matters 13, 140, 141–142
Extended Schools 141, 146

friendship *see* Circle of Friends
funding 36, 107, 108

games 44, 48–50, 53, 77
gender 30, 38
government initiatives 13, 140–147

Hartley-Brewer, E. 9, 142
health 28, 142–143
Hutson, N. 23, 30

identity 46, 62–63, 85
inclusion 92, 140; *see also* Circle of Friends

Jackins, H. 12, 26–27

Keele University Anti-bullying Project 28,
 124

Le Surf, P. 10
legal framework 112
listening *see* active listening; peer listening
Lynch, G. 10

mediators *see* peer mediation
Moldrich, C. 11, 25, 51, 108
Monitorial System 11
monitoring and evaluation 30, 39–40,
 118–120
 buddy room referral form 157
 collated review data 162
 impact evaluation 119
 peer mentor/mediator review 158–159
 post-course questionnaire 154–155, 156
 pre-course questionnaire 152–153, 156
 process evaluation 119

students' review of peer support 160–161
Morgan, D. 20

National Children's Bureau 131
National Curriculum 29, 140, 142,
 145–146
needs analysis 34–35
Newton, C. et al. 28, 91–92, 93, 96, 97, 98,
 99, 100, 101–102

paraphrasing 59
parents 38, 94–95, 97–98
peer advocacy 18
peer assessment 18, 117
peer assisted learning (PAL) 22
peer counselling 18–19, 28, 51–52, 63–64,
 143; *see also* co–counselling training
 course
peer education 19–20
peer listening 20, 28, 51–52, 55; *see also*
 co–counselling training course
peer mediation 12, 20, 28, 72–75, 143
 benefits 72, 143
 context 75
 contracts 90
 mediators 72
 programme planning 88
 prompt sheets 168–169
 review 158–159
 role 73–74, 79–80, 164
 role-play 86–87, 89, 170, 171–172
 stages 86
 training 72
 see also conflict resolution course
peer mentoring 20–21, 28, 52, 143
 case studies 21, 125, 126–127
 review 158–159
 see also co-counselling training course
peer relationships 26, 27
peer research 21–22
peer support
 applications 15–24
 benefits 10, 11, 28–29, 131
 core skills 39
 definitions 9–10
 history 11–13
 potential difficulties 29–30
 principles 15–16
 reasons for use 10–11
 research evidence 25, 28–30
 students' review 160–161
 theories 25–27
Peer Support Forum 13, 15–16, 23, 38,
 110